Praises For
Bite-size Devotions for the Busy Christian

Greetings from Zimbabwe, Southern Africa. My name is Karl Malotane. I am based in Zimbabwe but frequently travel focusing on Theological Education in Southern Africa (TCSA).

An extension of my key role as Academic Dean for Theological College of Southern Africa entails leading two online learning groups with students and church leaders mainly from Southern African countries. These are the two groups where we constantly post the devotions done by Pastor Terry Nightingale. There has and is some tremendous response from the leaders from the different denominations expressing their appreciation to how the devotions from his blog '4- minute devotions' have transformed their lives.

We therefore highly endorse his devotions, and I believe that this book *Bite-Size Devotions for the Busy Christian* will benefit the Church in Southern Africa as the body of Christ.

—**Karl Malotane** DipEd; BTh; BAHns;
MA Academic Dean, Theological College of Southern Africa

***

I always enjoy reading Terry's online 4-minute devotions. They inspire, encourage and challenge. A great way to start the day! And this book of similar devotions will prove of equal benefit to everyone who reads it. Highly recommended!

—**Graham Jefferson**, UK-based Baptist minister and itinerant Bible teacher.

***

With intensity and urgency, Terry Nightingale draws from both Old and New Testament Scriptures to lead readers into a closer relationship with Christ in *Bite-Size Devotions for the Busy Christian*.

—**Tracy Crump**, co-director of Write Life Workshops and author of *Health, Healing, and Wholeness: Devotions of Hope in the Midst of Illness*.

***

Terry Nightingale has a unique and expressive style that creates him to be a writer for this generation. I am absolutely delighted to find such a captivating arrangement of devotionals so carefully and lovingly prepared by Terry. Not only are they the most interesting devotionals you will EVER read, but you will also very suddenly become very attached to them. I thoroughly recommend these for your daily reading. They are so delicious, and like me you will be compelled to keep turning the pages. Terry – I thank God for the gift He has given you to write this wonderful Holy Spirit created book of Golden Nuggets.

—**Rev. Pastor Iris White**, Vice International Director TJG Int and Director UK – TJG Int
Executive Director Women of Faith Foundation Int.
Founder of online Thanet Christian Radio (Kent - UK)

***

It has been my privilege to share fellowship with Terry even though we live at opposite ends of the Globe. Through my friendship with Terry, I have been introduced to his 4-minute devotionals. Pithy, well thought out and theologically sound, three things that are difficult to do in bite-sized articles, Terry manages to do just that, and some. The message of the Gospel as well as a challenge and/or encouragement for the Christian believer, serves to make these devotionals, something to cheer the heart and feed the soul. Now they are available in this book form, *Bite-Size Devotions for the Busy Christian*, they will do the same.

I have sensed that these 'offerings' come from the heart of a man who walks in close fellowship with his LORD and Saviour, and thus they are the overflow of such a 'heart'.

—**Dr Charlie Sommerville**, Truth To Live By Ministries.

***

In a time of uncertainty, doubt, and gloomy darkness as the coronavirus swept across the world, creating quarantine, Terry Nightingale's heartfelt biblical four-minute devotions are refreshing rays of light. Terry's devotions are a blessing to my family.

Thank you, Terry, for your wholehearted biblical devotions. I am delighted that you are compiling this wonderful collection into a book to reach more people. Your devotions have been pure blessings to my family and me, especially during the coronavirus pandemic and quarantine. Your devotions have also kept me encouraged and uplifted during my studies in my Doctor of Ministry degree. It has been refreshing to have such awesome spiritual devotions to take my mind and focus off the troublesome/terrible happenings worldwide. I thank God for the time and dedication you contribute to your beautiful devotions. Your invigorating and encouraging four-minute godly devotions are a blessing to the world! I pray God continues to use you!

—**George W. Willett III**, Associate Pastor.

***

A year or so ago, I saw a blog of Terry Nightingale's and thoroughly enjoyed what he had written. I responded to it with a comment, which he appreciated very much. As a result of our connection, I started receiving his blog journals every time he posted them. I found the subjects of each of his blogs insightful, and at times they uniquely ministered to me at the most appropriate time or to a situation in my life. With each of the articles, Terry has graced us with the godly wisdom that can only come from the Holy Spirit, and his time spent seeking the Lord. What he shares will speak to anyone, no matter their gender, age, education, life experiences, geographical location, or social position, because they are rooted in the Word of God, which is timeless. As a pastor and shepherd of his flock, Terry has tapped into the mind, heart, and spirit of the Great Shepherd of the Church. Take the time to read, and meditate on each article, because they will enrich your life, mind, and soul. In the times that we now live, we need more than just what we hear in church on Sunday morning: we need continual input, and I know that this book will be a great blessing to you.

—**Keith D. Wilcox, D.M.A.**
Associate Pastor of Music and Worship
New Colony Baptist Church
Billerica, Massachusetts, USA

Bite-size Devotions for the Busy Christian

Terry Nightingale

Published by KHARIS PUBLISHING, imprint of KHARIS MEDIA LLC.

Copyright © 2021 Terry Nightingale

ISBN-13: 978-1-63746-075-7

ISBN-10: 1-63746-075-9

Library of Congress Control Number: 2021943937

All rights reserved. This book or parts thereof may not be reproduced in any form, stored in a retrieval system, or transmitted in any form by any means - electronic, mechanical, photocopy, recording, or otherwise - without prior written permission of the publisher, except as provided by United States of America copyright law.

All Scripture quotations, unless otherwise indicated, are taken from the Holy Bible, New International Version®, NIV®. Copyright ©1973, 1978, 1984, 2011 by Biblica, Inc.™ Used by permission.

All KHARIS PUBLISHING products are available at special quantity discounts for bulk purchase for sales promotions, premiums, fund-raising, and educational needs. For details, contact:

Kharis Media LLC

Tel: 1-479-599-8657

support@kharispublishing.com

www.kharispublishing.com

CONTENTS

Introduction	xi
Day 1 - The Most Amazing Thing about Angels	1
Day 2 - The Miracle of Forgiveness	3
Day 3 - Nothing is Impossible with God	5
Day 4 - Five Views, One Picture	7
Day 5 - A Powerful Prayer	9
Day 6 - In the Presence of My Enemies	11
Day 7 - A Passion for the Gospel	13
Day 8 - Grace for the Weak	15
Day 9 - Ask and You Shall Receive	17
Day 10 - On the Shoulders of History	19
Day 11 - I want to Know Christ	21
Day 12 - No Shame	23
Day 13 – Ecclesiastes	25
Day 14 - Possessing the Possessions	27
Day 15 - God Our Refuge	29
Day 16 - The Most Beautiful Thing I have ever Seen	31
Day 17 - Putting on the Right Clothes	33
Day 18 - Following Jesus	35
Day 19 - Forgiveness	37
Day 20 - The Next Step	39
Day 21 - The Place of Highest Authority	41

Day 22 – Family……………………………………………… 43

Day 23 - The Pharisee Within……………………………….. 45

Day 24 - Set Apart…………………………………………... 47

Day 25 - Gazing on the Beauty of the Lord………………….. 49

Day 26 - Wisdom and Knowledge…………………………… 51

Day 27 – Treasures…………………………………………... 53

Day 28 – Fruitfulness………………………………………… 55

Day 29 - Eating for the Glory of God………………………... 57

Day 30 – Watchmen………………………………………….. 59

Day 31 - Being Like-Minded………………………………… 61

Day 32 - How Much More…………………………………… 63

Day 33 - But I Grew up with this Guy……………………….. 65

Day 34 - God will do what He said He will do………………. 67

Day 35 - Looking Forward to Heaven……………………….. 69

Day 36 - Gathering and Reaping……………………………... 71

Day 37 – Truth……………………………………………….. 73

Day 38 - Looking for Peace………………………………….. 75

Day 39 - A Spacious Place…………………………………… 77

Day 40 - Bread and Wine…………………………………….. 79

Day 41 - God can use Anyone……………………………….. 81

Day 42 - He Watches over You……………………………… 83

Day 43 - Is the Lord's Arm too Short?……………………….. 85

Day 44 - He Delights in You…………………………………. 87

Day 45 - God Knows You by Name………………………….. 89

Day 46 - Content to be a Child…………………………………..	91
Day 47 - Being Fat for Jesus………………………………………..	93
Day 48 - Close to the Shepherd's Heart…………………………….	95
Day 49 - Deep Calls to Deep………………………………………..	97
Day 50 - Barriers to Faith……………………………………………..	99
Day 51 - Be Strong and Take Heart………………………………...	101
Day 52 - All That for Just One Person…………………………….	103
Day 53 - Go Back to the Mountain………………………………..	105
Day 54 - Hold Your Ground………………………………………..	107
Day 55 – Grace………………………………………………………..	109
Day 56 - On Things Above………………………………………...	111
Day 57 – Intercessors…………………………………………………	113
Day 58 - The Best Way to Memorise Scripture…………………..	115
Day 59 - How Great is Your God?………………………………...	117
Day 60 - A People Who Bless……………………………………...	119
Day 61 - Two Incarnations………………………………………….	121
Day 62 - The Trinity Verses………………………………………....	123
Day 63 - You Give Them Something to Eat…………………….	125
Day 64 - I Will Give You Rest……………………………………....	127
Day 65 - Talking to Myself…………………………………………	129
Day 66 - Reach out a Hand………………………………………...	131
Day 67 - The 'One Another' Scriptures………………………….	133
Day 68 - The Unforgivable Sin…………………………………...	135
Day 69 - Unless the Lord Builds the House……………………...	137

Day 70 - Trembling before God's Word................................... 139

Day 71 - Carrying Burdens... 141

Day 72 - Dealing with Guilt.. 143

Day 73 – Generosity... 145

Day 74 – Purity.. 147

Day 75 – Peace.. 149

Day 76 – Purpose... 151

Day 77 - The Secret of Joy... 153

Day 78 - The Most Creative People on the Planet.................... 155

Day 79 - Walking in Reverse.. 157

Day 80 - Eternal Life.. 159

INTRODUCTION

Bare Feet, The Beatles and the Bible as God-breathed

In September 1969, the English rock group The Beatles released their album, *Abbey Road*, with the iconic photo of the four members of the band walking across a zebra crossing in London NW8.

For some time prior to this album, stories had been circulating that bassist and vocalist, Paul McCartney had died in a car crash and that an imposter was replacing him. The 'Paul is dead' rumour became one of the biggest hoaxes of the year, unwittingly fueled by the album cover.

For some, the photo provided definitive proof that the musician really had died. For starters John Lennon wore a white suit, symbolizing the colour of mourning in some eastern religions, while Ringo Starr donned the more traditional black. McCartney held a cigarette in his right hand even though he was a lefty (thus, proving he was an imposter!). A car in the picture had a '28' on the number plate – the age Paul would be if he were alive, and the black police van symbolised the authorities who had apparently kept the accident a secret.

And then there was Paul's bare feet – in some cultures the dead are buried without their shoes. Paul must be dead, they said; the bare feet are telling us that.

Almost 50 years later in 2018 the then 76-year-old musician was asked why he posed for the photo in with no shoes or socks on. "The thing was I turned up and, like today, it was a very hot day," he said.

Sometimes the simplest explanations are the right ones.

In the previous year, 1968, the Beatles had released a double record popularly known as *The White Album*. Across the Atlantic in a place known as Death Valley in California, a cult leader, Charles Manson had bought a copy and had begun listening to it. Over and over. He came to believe that the lyrics of the songs had been written for him. Just him. John, Paul and George, the main writers of the songs were apparently singing about Manson, his thoughts and ideas.

Of course, this was far from the truth and the Beatles had never met or heard of the Manson family, but as far as Charles was concerned, *The White Album*, confirmed and gave permission to him to carry out a series of brutal murders. One song in particular, *Helter Skelter*, set the terrible chain of events in motion.

It goes without saying that every one of the four Beatles were as shocked as the rest of the world, and horrified that their songs could be used as justification for violence. Words written for fun and entertainment had been terribly misinterpreted to create meanings unintended by the original writers.

Interestingly, Charles Manson also did that with the Bible, specifically the book of Revelation. Of course, many have speculated as to the meanings of the numerous phrases and images in the last book of the Bible, but Manson must take the gold prize for the strangest. From 'horses prepared for battle' (Rev 9: 7) referring to his family's dune buggies to locusts being the Beatles themselves, Manson took Biblical interpretation to a whole new level.

Which brings us to the study of Hermeneutics – the interpretation of literary texts. I remember, years ago, sitting in a series of Bible studies conducted by a friend of mine, also through the book of Revelation. My friend (who I will call Eric) has a doctorate in Theology and is as far from the mind of Charles Manson as California is to London, but I noticed something about his approach to Revelation that I found intriguing. And, as much as I respect my friend, I couldn't agree with it.

To set the scene, the writer of Revelation (who I will assume to be John the youngest disciple of Jesus), tells us in the first verse that the 'Revelation' is something God *gave* him. A loud voice said to him, "Write on a scroll what you see" (Rev 1: 11) and later, "Write, therefore, what you have seen, what is now and what will take place later" (1: 19). John's job was to watch a series of unfolding scenes, try to describe them in words and write down what he hears.

And John faithfully did that job: 'After this I looked' (Rev 4: 1); 'Then I saw…' (5: 1); 'I watched as the lamb…' (6: 1) etc. I was puzzled therefore when my friend continually asked throughout the course, "What do you think

John meant by this word, phrase, image… etc?" On day one, I offered the thought that John meant *nothing* – he was simply writing down what he saw. That's what he was supposed to do, right? Eric ignored me every time I made that point.

I believe to this day that my friend, who is far smarter and more qualified than I, failed to see something of vital importance in the world of Biblical interpretation – the 'plain meaning of the text'.

In legal terms, traditionally applied by British courts, the plain meaning rule dictates that words and sentences are to be interpreted using the ordinary meaning of the language. In other words, when we read things, let's not discard common sense. The most obvious meaning is probably the right one.

And this is what I have tried to do with the devotions in the book you are now holding. Let the Bible speak and seek the plain meaning of the text. Receive it as God's inspired Word, read it in context and try not to overcomplicate things.

Paul describes Scripture as 'God-breathed' in 2 Tim 3: 16. He was probably referring to the Hebrew Scriptures (the Old Testament to you and me) but may also have had in mind the community memory of Jesus' parables and sayings. Peter also mentions Paul's letters in one of his own (in 2 Pet 3: 15 – 16) describing them as Scripture. The plain meaning of all of this is that the Bible has come from God, He inspired humans to write down each part and we can trust it as coming from Him.

So, when it comes to interpretation, let's read the stories as they are, receive the words as a gift from God, hear the words as they speak (mostly) plainly and soak them in a bucket of common sense. The simplest meanings of the stories are probably the right ones.

As you read these devotions, I hope they are a blessing to you. Feel free to ignore my own thoughts or ideas but do me a favour: Let the Words of Scripture speak plainly to you and welcome them into your heart.

DAY 1

The Most Amazing Thing about Angels

Here are the basic facts (according to the Scriptures): They exist. They are created beings, made by God. They have the ability to make moral choices (see 2 Pet 2: 24). They can speak and interact with people, so, for example, when Peter was set free from prison by an angel in Acts 5: 19 - 20, he was given specific instructions to continue his work of preaching and teaching.

Next, they are invisible to us until God makes them visible. I love the story in 2 Kings 6: 8 – 17. Here we find the king of Israel and his prophet Elisha in the city of Dotham, surrounded by a formidable army with horses and chariots. One servant voiced the fears of many as he asked, 'what will we do?'

'Don't be afraid,' the prophet answered. 'Those who are with us are more than those who are with them,' and he proceeded to pray for eyes to be opened. In a moment, the servant saw an even bigger army surrounded by fire. This brings us to our next fact: They have great power. They are the 'mighty ones' in Psalm 103: 20 and those who are 'stronger and more powerful' than humans in 2 Pet 2: 11.

But there is one thing more mind-blowing than all of this, something far more incredible. Simply this – *they serve us*!

Think about it. We are the ones who have disobeyed God, we are the ones who have misused His holy name, and our sins drove the nails into the hands and feet of God's holy Son. Compare that to the angels who dwell in the holy presence of God and who have done nothing wrong. The angels have power and abilities beyond our wildest dreams, yet they work for *our* good and for *our* protection. According to the book of Hebrews, angels are ministering spirits sent to serve those who will inherit salvation – us!

Why on earth would we be so privileged?

The Bible provides us with some answers. The first is found at the beginning in the book of Genesis. At the end of each of the first five days of creation, God steps back, surveys the scene and declares it good, but after creating humans, His approval rating has stepped up to 'very good' (Gen 1: 31). He has made us in His own image and given us dominion over everything else.

The writer of Psalm 8 reflects on this. We were made a little lower than the angels (v 5). That is, we are of the dust of the earth, yet we are crowned with glory and honour. We rule as His kingly representatives.

By the time we get to the New Testament, Christ's death on the cross and resurrection has rendered us (by repentance and faith) new creations 'in Christ' (1 Cor 1: 2), 'raised up' with Him and 'seated with him in the heavenly realms' (Eph 2: 5). We are permanently in the place of highest authority.

We have done nothing to deserve this, of course, but next time you are tempted to look down upon yourself or live less than God's best for you, remember who He has made you to be – children of God, made in the image of God and seated with Christ in the heavenly realms.

Even the angels serve you.

Suggested Prayer: "Lord, thank you that I am made in your image, and by faith in you and your death on the cross, I am now a new creation and seated with you in the heavenly realms. I am proud to be one of your children. Please help me to live as a child of God in my thoughts, words and actions. Amen."

DAY 2

The Miracle of Forgiveness

I wonder if you have read the remarkable story in Mark chapter two, where a crowd of people listening to Jesus speaking in a house were surprised by the interruption of a paralyzed man being lowered through the roof to his feet. As the makeshift stretcher slowly descended, all eyes would have been on the man, then on Jesus, then back on the man. What will Jesus do? Every person present would surely have hoped to see a miracle right in front of their eyes.

But Jesus doesn't heal him, at least not straight away. All He does is tell the young man that his sins are forgiven.

The teachers of the law, who have likely travelled from Jerusalem to be there are immediately critical: 'This is blasphemy! Who can forgive sins but God alone?' (2: 7). Why would Jesus do this? He seems to be deliberately walking into conflict.

The Gospels, of course, are full of accounts of Jesus' actions and sayings that intentionally point to His true identity – Emmanuel, God with us. So, Jesus, just to make clear to His audience that He does in fact have divine authority to pronounce forgiveness over the man, confirms it by also healing him. No wonder people in the crowd said, "we have never seen anything like this" (2: 12)

But I think there is another reason why Jesus forgave the man's sins. Matthew's version of the story has Jesus saying, *"take heart son*, your sins are forgiven" (Matt 9: 2). Somehow Jesus felt He needed to speak to the man with deep compassion - as if He knew the man was weighed down with guilt. Perhaps the young man even believed that he deserved his physical condition because of something he had done. The text doesn't give answers to these speculations, but I suggest that there are hints in Jesus' words that what the man desperately needed was a clean conscience. And only God can give that.

When Jesus heals it is always a miracle, but perhaps His forgiveness is a miracle too. The once-paralyzed man walked away free from his physical suffering but also free from his guilt. I'm surprised we don't see him skipping to a tune on his way out – maybe the dancing happened with his family later!

1 John 1: 9 tells us that if we confess our sins to Him, then He, being just and faithful will forgive us our sins. We all know what it feels like to carry a burden of guilt. We can try and hide it, suppress it, even try to justify the actions that caused it, but we can't set ourselves free from it. Only forgiveness from the one who has authority to forgive will work.

Is Jesus challenging you to repent of something? Have you been carrying a weight that you can't shake off? Perhaps He wants to give you a miracle today – the miracle of forgiveness.

Suggested prayer: "Lord, thank you for the fact that you are a God of deep compassion. You don't delight in pointing out our sin, but you love us enough to do so, so that we might receive your forgiveness and enjoy a new start. Lord, I am sorry for the things I have done wrong. Please forgive me and wash me clean. Amen."

DAY 3

Nothing is Impossible with God

Have you ever been backed into a corner? Or felt that way. You're in a sticky situation with no way out.

The Israelites must have felt that way when they faced the Red Sea.

When God led the Israelites out of Egypt, they were not an army. They were tribes and families. In fact, the Lord deliberately avoided a route through Philistine country (which would have been shorter) because 'if they face war, they might change their minds and return to Egypt' (Ex 13: 17).

So, imagine men, untrained for battle, yet nervously holding anything that might pass as a weapon, alongside their wives and children, realizing that a highly trained and cruel Egyptian fighting force are bearing down on them, with desert on either side and a vast body of water in front of them.

They were literally caught between the devil and the deep blue sea.

Most people know the rest of the Bibles' most famous story. Under the Lord's command, Moses, standing at the waters edge, stretched out his hand over the sea, which promptly parted. The stunned Israelites walked across a dry seabed, but as the Egyptian army pursued them Moses lifted his hand again, and tons of water crashed back into place crushing every soldier and chariot.

What strikes me about this story is how God *created* an answer to their prayers. His solution was original, to say the least, and completely unexpected.

Of course, many have speculated *how* God might have wrought this miracle, with explanations ranging from Tsunamis to quirks within fluid dynamics to a phenomenon known as 'wind setdown' (the text tells us that 'the Lord drove the sea back with a strong east wind' – 14: 21). There does seem to be a tendency among us humans to want to try and explain supernatural things in natural terms.

The point I want to make though is that, at the exact moment of greatest need, a miracle occurred completely out of left field. No-one saw it coming! At the point where no person could see a way out of their calamitous situation, God re-wrote the rules of nature and triumphantly presented a new solution. He not only provided a way of escape for the Israelites; He also completely destroyed the threat on their backs.

Sometimes I try to imagine how God might answer my prayers, but then I only see limits instead of the infinite possibilities. I try to look at logical solutions to my problems but forget that God's brain is bigger than mine. Even when I try to think outside the box for a way forward, I fail to remember that God is more than able to get rid of the box altogether!

It goes without saying that God often uses the natural for His purposes. We know that! We rightly pray that He will act through the expertise of surgeons when a loved one is facing an operation and we know that He invented the laws of science. We know that God gave us extraordinary abilities to design and make and build, but how easy it is to only look there.

If our Lord is a creator, then can He not also bring a solution out of nowhere? I think so, because nothing is impossible with God.

Suggested prayer: "Lord, thank you because with you there are always endless possibilities. You are the God of creative miracles. When I don't see solutions, you do. When I can't see a way forward, I can remind myself that nothing is impossible with God. Amen."

DAY 4

Five Views, One Picture

Like many Christians, I go to church. I have to, I'm the pastor! But to be honest, even if I wasn't on staff, I would still choose to be part of a local community of believers, despite the fact we don't always get it right.

However, current statistics show that many who identify themselves as Christian prefer not to attend church services. Some may choose the increasing online options; some don't feel the need; sadly, some have had a negative church experience and would rather stay away.

The amazing thing is that, even though humans have made many mistakes - sometimes even devastating failures – the Church and local congregations still remain God's plan A.

And, as far as we know, there is no plan B!

God has always had hope for the Church, believing she can be who she was created to be and describes her with beautiful, vivid, metaphors: for example, a bride. Jesus is the bridegroom, and we are the betrothed. At the end of time, the multitude of believers in Jesus Christ will burst into celebration with the words, 'Let us rejoice and be glad and give him glory! For the wedding of the Lamb has come, and his bride has made herself ready' (Rev 19: 7 – 8). The vast crowd can do nothing but worship at the reminder and fresh realisation that they are the object of God's love.

In other places in Scripture, Jesus has described himself as a shepherd, but think about that for a moment! 'I am the good shepherd', said Jesus, 'The good shepherd lays down his life for the sheep' (John 10: 11). Therefore we, as the Church, are the flock of God, rescued and gathered, known intimately by name, guided and protected by the One who suffered death on a cross for us. The Church reveals a glimpse of God's care for His children.

In Ephesians 2, the church is likened to a temple (Eph 2: 21), the place where the ancient Israelites experienced God's presence. As we gather today in Jesus' name, God is pleased to dwell among us.

The Bible describes the church as a vine, engrafted into *the* Vine - Jesus, and in a passage that seems to admit we don't always get it right, branches are cut off and branches are pruned. The Lord disciplines, so that the vine 'will be even more fruitful' (John 15: 2). What does it mean to be fruitful? Perhaps that is best answered by the fifth description of the church.

In Colossians 1: 15, 18, Jesus is described as the image of the invisible God and the head of 'the body' – the church. The church is like a human body, *His* body in fact. 'you are the body of Christ, and each one of you is a part of it' (1 Cor 12: 27). As His body, as His hands and feet, we go into the world with the good news of Jesus Christ and the blessings of Heaven. 'If your gift is prophesying, then prophesy in accordance with your faith; if it is serving, then serve; if it is teaching, then teach; if it is to encourage, then give encouragement; if it is giving, then give generously; if it is to lead, do it diligently; if it is to show mercy, do it cheerfully' (Rom 12: 6 – 8).

Five views that form one beautiful picture. The Church is still God's A plan – deeply loved like a husband loves his bride, rescued, cared for and guided. God is present every time she gathers but is unafraid to bring correction and discipline in order that we, together, might be His hands and feet in a dying world.

God has never stopped desiring that the church be a place of His Love, His care and His presence. She was called to be God's hands and feet to the wider community where she will bear His fruit. For our part, can we strive to be anything less?

Suggested prayer: Lord, thank you that you created the church. We know we don't always get it right and some have even had negative experiences within the context of church life. Lord, I pray for church leaders around the globe, for those in my country, in my city and in my church. Help them to lead and serve congregations in ways that reflect your love, truth and care. Amen.

DAY 5

A Powerful Prayer

Imagine you are on a beach and you pick up a handful of sand. How many grains of sand do you see? 100? 500? A lot more, probably. It would be difficult to count them.

So, if someone were to ask us to estimate the number of grains along the *whole* beach, I for one would not know where to start. It's immeasurable – too big to know.

When Paul writes to the Ephesian Christians in the book of Ephesians (3: 20) he reminds them that God can do more than they are asking for in prayer. And not just more, but *immeasurably* more – like grains of sand on a beach. Actually, he says, God can do more than *all* we ask for. In fact, continues Paul, let your mind go wild for a second, even more than anything you can imagine. That's how much God is able to meet your need or answer your prayer.

But it's the last part of the verse that blows my mind. Paul writes, '…according to His power that is at work within us'. It is the Spirit of God working in us, and through us, that is able to do so much more than we pray for, or even expect. Because He is a Spirit of power.

Let's talk about God's power for a moment. Going back to verse 16, Paul lets the believers in Ephesus (and beyond) in on a secret: he tells them what he prays for them. He prays that they will be strengthened with God's power. He prays that the Holy Spirit will have free reign even in the deepest recesses of their hearts, 'I pray… He may strengthen you with power through His Spirit in your inner being'.

He prays power for them again in verse 18. He wants them to have the power to be able to 'grasp how wide and how long and high and deep is the love of Christ' (v 18). Why? Well, in the verse leading up to this, he wants them 'rooted and established' in Christ's love.

Roots from large, mature trees spread far and wide, some dig down deep as far as 100 feet (30m) or more. Roots can even grow through rock. They transport water and essential minerals to the trunk and branches and, of course, anchor the tree to stand firm against the wind.

Paul prays that the church will find that essential root system in Christ's love. That's a powerful prayer to pray ourselves today – that, consciously and unconsciously, our sustenance (the essential minerals of God's Word), our water supply (the daily infilling of the Holy Spirit) and our strength (the ability to stand firm through the storm), come out of, and directly from a grasp of one simple truth: He loves me! His love for us is infinite in all directions, even beyond my ability to fathom it out (v 19).

I don't know about you, but I don't mind admitting that I need His power. And I need to be aware of the power that is already within me, by His Holy Spirit. Maybe, once we get our heads around that one, we can, along with St Paul, declare that the Lord is indeed, 'able to do immeasurably more than all we ask or imagine, according to His power that is at work within us'.

Suggested Prayer: Reflect on Eph 3: 20 and the wonderful truth that God can do immeasurably more than all we ask or imagine. Then go back a few verses to v 14 – 19. Pray each verse for yourself and for those in your care.

DAY 6

In the Presence of My Enemies

When was the last time you felt under spiritual attack?

Paul reminded the Ephesian Christians that they were, 'not fighting against flesh-and-blood enemies, but against evil rulers and authorities of the unseen world, against mighty powers in this dark world, and against evil spirits in the heavenly places' (Eph 6: 12, NLT).

Spiritual attack can strike the believer in many ways or sneak up on us in a variety of disguises. They may come in the form of a discouragement or a sense of opposition They may be behind an unexpected trouble or breakdown in a relationship. Our enemy, the devil might cloak himself in a temptation or a feeling of darkness entering your soul. You only have to be a Christian for five minutes to realise that the enemy doesn't like it!

That is why the Psalms are so helpful to us. David's honest prayers often reveal the depths of his heart during a time of physical threat or attack. He then points the reader towards his Saviour. What David faced with flesh-and-blood enemies is a reality for us in the spiritual realm. If God can help David, He can help us.

The remarkable thing about Psalm 23 is that David has found peace, 'in the presence of my enemies' (v 5). He has conquered his fear, even though he walks, 'through the valley of the shadow of death' (v 4); and he has discovered a place to, 'lie down in green pastures' even in the midst of the battlefield (v 2).

David, who was a shepherd in his youth, sees the Lord as the ultimate Shepherd leading him, guiding him and restoring him. God gently disciplines him and points the way with His rod and staff (v 4), but David also recognizes the enormity of God's grace. David knows God's love as a sheep under the Shepherd's care, but he also rejoices in His place as an honored guest in the Lord's house.

'You prepare a table before me
in the presence of my enemies.
You anoint my head with oil;
my cup overflows.' (Ps 23: 5)

This is a great reminder for us. Look where you are seated when the enemy feels nearby! As sheep, we are under the loving care of the shepherd, but as children of God we are invited to dine at the King's table. The Good Shepherd (John 10: 11) is our royal host and He has prepared a feast – the riches of grace from Heaven's endless resources. He loves to anoint our heads with oil (He fills us with His Spirit), and He fills our cup to overflowing every time we lift our hands in prayer to Him.

Next time you feel the spiritual attack, stop and take in your surroundings. You may be on the battlefield, but you are also in the banquet hall of the King.

Suggested prayer: "Lord, when I feel under spiritual attack, I want to put my focus on you. Thank you that I am always under your loving care but thank you that I am also near your throne and in your banquet hall. You give me everything I need, and you fill me to overflowing. Amen"

DAY 7

A Passion for the Gospel

What do you love most about being a Christian? The peace, the joy, the sense of purpose? Being part of a faith community?

Many would answer the fellowship, the love and care they have for one another. Some might describe their new life in Christ as one wonderfully different to the path they once followed. Hopefully, all of us would talk about our new relationship with God and how thankful we are to Him for the things He is doing in our lives.

But how much do we love sharing the Gospel – or even thinking about it? We are, of course, grateful for Christ's death on the cross and humbled by the sacrifice He made for us, but how much does that translate into deep reflection and real, effective action? Is it a tag-on to the fun we have with Christian friends or is it at the core of everything we do?

'I am not ashamed of the Gospel', wrote the apostle Paul, 'because it is the power of God that brings salvation to everyone who believes' (Rom 1: 16).

Paul knew what it was like to develop close bonds with others throughout the churches he planted. He described his 'intense longing' to see those in his care separated from him for a season (1 Thess 2: 17), and he made a long list of special friends and fellow workers in the sixteenth chapter of Romans, but he never stopped putting the Gospel first in his heart and in his life. Even when he was locked up in prison the uppermost thing in his mind was that the gospel would not be hindered: 'The important thing is that in every way, whether from false motives or true, Christ is preached' (Phil 1: 17).

Someone once said, 'the church exists for the benefit of its non-members'. I am challenged by that. There are so many things I love about being a Christian but, at the end of the day, there is a world out there full of people who are yet to experience a loving relationship with their Father in Heaven. And if we don't make the introduction, who will?

We may not all be evangelists, but we can pray for the lost; we may not all have the gift of the gab, but we can be a friend to someone who needs God; we may not feel we are that good at articulating spiritual things, but we can tell our story and we can invite our friend to an event where the Gospel will be preached by someone who does have that gift.

Do you love the Gospel? Do you love it as much as the benefits and blessings of being a Christian? Let us ask the Lord to rekindle a passion for the Gospel in our hearts – and to keep asking. There is a world out there that needs His message more than ever.

Suggested prayer: find a piece of paper or a new page on your electronic device. Start listing people you know (ask the Holy Spirit to help you) who are not yet Christians. It can be a sizable list or just one or two. Try to pray for some (or even one) every day. Pray that they might hear the Gospel; pray that God will give them the faith to believe.

DAY 8

Grace for the Weak

One of my cats is a chicken!

I'm not saying that he lays eggs, more that he seems to lack any kind of courage when it counts.

Both of our cats were being terrorised by another meaner feline, who had come to take over the neighborhood. Our older cat (Toosy – don't ask!), stood guard by our front door every night like an indomitable soldier on sentry duty. The younger one, Reho, scarpered every time fur appeared.

Now, years later, Toosy is old, and hobbles around the house at half impulse while Reho still vanishes at the sound of anything sudden. The sad thing, though, is that the one cat Reho does attack is the frail Toosy – the one who used to protect him from the local bully.

Toosy has become weak, but Reho has no grace for him.

King David is one of the most fascinating characters in the Bible. He was tough but real. He was deeply flawed, yet very human and with a heart that pleased God.

There is an interesting story in 1 Samuel chapter 30. David, before he became king, faced a terrible situation when his family and the families of his private army were captured by the Amalekites. An immediate rescue was planned but having recently returned from a long journey, 200 of his men were too exhausted to follow him back into battle. The remaining 400 went with him to face a much bigger army.

Miraculously, all returned with no-one harmed and they were even able to loot the enemy soldiers. But as they approached the place where they had left the 200, the murmuring started. 'They don't deserve any of the plunder. We did the hard yards, so we get the rewards. They can take their families (who *we* rescued, by the way) and go.' 'We don't have time for weak people'.

The 400 said that the 200 did not deserve any of loot because they had not taken part in the fight. To their great surprise, David disagreed. Rather than condemn the 200 for their weakness caused by severe exhaustion, he reminded the 400 that the victory was actually a gift from God Himself. God had given them grace; therefore, maybe the 400 should give grace to their fellow soldiers.

I wonder if you can think of someone who doesn't deserve something. Maybe you feel they don't deserve forgiveness or a second chance; what they've done persuades you to hold back your acceptance or friendship. Maybe they haven't proved themselves worthy to receive rewards or blessings. They haven't earned our love, so we are within our rights to walk away!

I find it helpful to remember that everything we have and everything I am is actually a gift – I don't deserve any of it. It is grace from God and God never holds back - grace comes to me in bucket-loads and if the Lord has given me so much of the stuff, perhaps I should start giving grace to others.

Suggested prayer. Did anybody come to mind as you read this story? Someone, perhaps, who has let you down. Someone you would rather not forgive. Take a few moments to lift them to the Lord. Express your own struggles honestly but ask God to help you to pray for them. Close your eyes, picture them in your mind and then pray for them as the Spirit leads.

DAY 9

Ask and You Shall Receive

I have so many needs right now, I don't know what to do

'...You do not have because you do not ask God' (James 4: 2b).

Ok, but how do I know that He will answer my prayer?

'Ask and it will be given to you; seek and you will find; knock and the door will be opened to you. For everyone who asks receives; the one who seeks finds; and to the one who knocks, the door will be opened' (Matt 7: 7 – 8).

Everyone? But I am nobody. Why would God be interested in me?

'Which of you, if your (child) asks for bread, will give him a stone? Or if he asks for a fish, will give him a snake? If you, then, though you are evil, know how to give good gifts to your children, how much more will your Father in heaven give good gifts to those who ask him!' (Matt 7: 9 – 11)

I don't feel that I have much faith. How much faith is enough?

'If you have faith as small as a mustard seed, you can say to this mulberry tree, "Be uprooted and planted in the sea," and it will obey you' (Luke 17: 6).

Really? Just a tiny amount of faith?

'Truly I tell you, if you have faith and do not doubt… you can say to this mountain, "Go, throw yourself into the sea" and it will be done. If you believe, you will receive whatever you ask for in prayer' (Matt 21: 21 - 22).

So, I can ask God for a big house and a fast car and He will give them to me?

'When you ask, you do not receive, because you ask with wrong motives, that you may spend what you get on your pleasures' (James 4: 2b – 3).

Oh right! So, I can't ask for things with the wrong motives and I'm guessing that I also can't keep doing those things that I know are wrong?

'Dear friends, if our hearts do not condemn us, we have confidence before God and receive from him anything we ask, because we keep his commands and do what pleases him' (1 John 3: 21 – 22).

Yeah, but I've tried all this. I didn't ask with the wrong motives, I wasn't aware of disobeying God in any way, but I still didn't get what I prayed for.

'And this is the confidence that we have toward him, that if we ask anything according to his will he hears us' (1 John 5: 14).

Maybe my friend will help me discern His will and pray for the things I need. Is that ok?

'…truly I tell you that if two of you on earth agree about anything they ask for, it will be done for them by my Father in heaven. For where two or three gather in my name, there am I with them' (Matt 18: 19).

I just need to pray and believe, right?

'…believe that you have received it, and it will be yours' (Mark 11: 24).

Suggested prayer: Bring your requests to God, He always hears you. Check your heart, check your motives and ask God to reveal His will to you. Perhaps find a friend to pray with, particularly if you are praying about something that involves a big decision.

DAY 10

On the Shoulders of History

Why do you trust God?

Perhaps you can remember times when you prayed, and He answered. Maybe you can articulate why the Bible is God's Word and why its promises still give hope today.

David reflects on God's faithfulness during a particularly difficult point in his life in Psalm 22. 'From birth I was cast on you; from my mother's womb you have been my God' (Ps 22: 10). God brought him into the world and even as a suckling newborn his dependence was on Him (v 9).

David looks to God because he always has, and because God has never let him down.

There is no context to point to in this psalm, although there are plenty of occurrences in David's life that might have inspired it. For sure though, he is in terrible danger, and David describes, as only he can, with vivid imagery the desperate situation he is in.

Enemy warriors are like strong bulls and roaring lions. Fear has gripped his heart, his strength is gone, and he feels trapped, encircled by evil (v 12 – 18). 'My mouth is dried up like a potsherd (like sun-baked clay), and my tongue sticks to the roof of my mouth; you lay me in the dust of death' (v 15).

Despite all this, and even despite the mocking laughter of those who try to tell him that God has abandoned him (v 6 – 8), David cries out to God.

Why does he do this, especially at a time when God seems to be silent?

I think an important answer is found in verses 4 – 5: 'In you our ancestors put their trust; they trusted, and you delivered them. To you they cried out and were saved; in you they trusted and were not put to shame'. This isn't about just God and me, says David, this isn't about my feelings or my circumstances. Or the silence. My faith is rooted in Israel's history – and you can't change that. It's rock solid and permanent.

I imagine David in his darkest moments recalling the stories of his youth: Abraham and his wife were well beyond child-bearing age, yet miraculously God gave them a son. Moses, a man afraid to speak in public, led the Israelites out of oppressive Egyptian rule amidst powerful signs and wonders. Joshua conquered city after city, slaying experienced battle-hardened soldiers and storming fortified cities in the power of the Lord.

It is the history of God's faithfulness that fuels David's trust in Him.

Yes, David expresses his trust out of personal experience. He has a testimony of God's love and care for him. But he roots his faith in the unchanging vaults of his nation's history. It happened back then, so God will be faithful now. The stories that define his people are fixed and set in stone, and so God will not let him down today.

Every time we pray today, we stand on the shoulders of history. Our testimony of God is precious and unique to each one of us, but we can continue to trust Him because generation after generation before us have found Him to be faithful.

Suggested prayer: Lord, thank you that many before me have found you to be faithful. I don't base my faith on how I feel today, but on the same Biblical truths that generation after generation before me have trusted in. Thank you that your promises are rock solid and permanent. Amen.

DAY 11

I want to Know Christ

In Philippians 3: 5 - 6, Paul lists all his religious privileges and achievements: he had been born into the tribe of Benjamin, then circumcised according to the law; he was a Hebrew through and through, in fact, he was an extremely zealous Pharisee, ambitious and faultless in his observance of the law.

If anyone was destined for greatness, it was Paul. A student of Gamaliel (Acts 22: 3), who was a leading authority of the Sanhedrin, Paul was educated, skilled in using animal skins to make tents, and he was raised in the important intellectual centre of the Roman Empire, Tarsus.

Yet, as he reflected on Christ's humility – the one who would not regard his equality with God the Father as something to be exploited (Phil 2: 6) and the one who made himself 'nothing' in human terms (2: 7) – Paul, too, laid aside everything that might be considered for his advantage: 'Whatever was to my profit I now consider loss for the sake of Christ' (3: 7).

Paul had found a new goal in life, a new driving passion: 'I consider everything a loss compared to the surpassing greatness of knowing Christ Jesus my Lord...' (3: 8), 'I want to know Christ and the power of his resurrection' (v 10).

Paul, of course, still used his privileges and abilities for the Kingdom of God as the Holy Spirit led him. He didn't abandon them altogether, but he refused to put his confidence in them for fruitful service. He determined to spend the rest of his life growing in his knowledge of Jesus and putting his complete trust in Him and His power.

I wonder what it meant for Paul (and, therefore, for us) to 'know' Christ? As far as we know, Paul had never met him in person. He had heard Jesus' voice on that, now famous, day in history when the Lord had stopped him on the Damascus Road, but he did not share the experiences of Peter, James and John who had travelled with Jesus, talking of all manner of things along long, dusty roads; sharing the same bread during countless meals together; watching, with awe, the miracles, and feeling the bitter experience of the cross.

But despite 'missing out' on those things, Paul still believed he could grow in his 'knowing' of Christ whilst serving Him on planet Earth, even though Christ's physical presence was no longer there. He also prayed that others, for example the Ephesian Christians, might know Jesus, especially His love (Eph 3: 17 – 18). What did he mean?

To know anyone well requires time, and shared experiences. Paul may not have lived and worked with Jesus in physical form, but we know that his dependence on Him through prayer was off the charts. His prayers of thanks were clearly part of his daily routine, overflowing many times into his letters (e.g., Col 1: 3, 2 Thess 1: 3). He was a man who yearned to be 'at home with the Lord (2 Cor 5: 8), regularly worshipping, rejoicing, and interceding with 'all kinds of prayers' (Eph 6: 18).

Every experience for Paul was intimately tied into his relationship with God; every journey and decision was made in consultation with his Lord and Saviour. Paul lived and breathed prayerful communion with Jesus. Perhaps that is one secret of knowing Christ.

Suggested prayer: "Lord, I want to know you more, to have prayerful communion with you throughout the day. I want to learn what it means to pray all kinds of prayers. Please help me to turn to you, not just with every important decision, but in everything I do. Amen."

DAY 12

No Shame

'In you, Lord my God, I put my trust.
I trust in you; do not let me be put to shame,
nor let my enemies triumph over me.
No one who hopes in you
will ever be put to shame' (Ps 25: 1 - 3)

Ancient Israel lived in an honour and shame society; to be 'put to shame' was no small matter.

For Mary to be 'found with child' at the beginning of the Christmas story, she would have known that she faced the very real possibility of being accused of adultery. To be accused of unfaithfulness and adultery in the 21st century is shameful enough, but in New Testament times, it was devastating.

The woman might be scourged; she would likely lose property, and she would certainly suffer public humiliation (see John 8: 3). Joseph, the man engaged to Mary, must have been a deeply compassionate and forgiving man because, even before his own visit from the angel in a dream, we are told he did not want to 'expose her to public disgrace' (Matt 1: 19).

To be 'put to shame' therefore meant, at the very least, to be exposed to public dishonour – a devaluing of a person in the eyes of family and immediate community. David's declaration of trust in Psalm 25 makes it clear that he expected to avoid the deep embarrassment of defeat by an enemy as he puts his hope in God. In David's eyes, trust in God meant honour, not shame.

But how does this work in the New Testament? When Jesus went to the cross, he suffered the ultimate public dishonour of being stripped naked, tortured and lifted up by nails before the entire city. Many of Jesus' followers suffered similar humiliation. Over the last two thousand years, some have also been publicly killed, or, at the very least, treated in such a way as to deliberately shame. Does this promise in the psalm no longer apply?

Corinth was an honour-shame society in Paul's day and young believers in Jesus in that city might still have been tempted to build aspects of their lives on those values – to present themselves and evaluate others in terms of physical appearance, status, personal success, and a desired reputation among the wider community.

However, Paul is clear in his re-definition of 'honour'. God did not choose the strong or the successful, but rather the weak and the foolish in the eyes of the world (1Cor 1: 27). Paul had first met the Corinthians, not as a skilled orator, or a bard entertaining with beautiful poetry. He had not arrived as travelling sage with impressive knowledge or wisdom. He came in fear and with trembling knees. But, just as Christ's humiliating death led to a powerful resurrection, Pauls' shame, in the eyes of the Corinthians, opened a door for the Spirit of God to work powerfully in their lives.

Later, when Paul refers to Psalm 25: 3 in Romans 10:11, he doesn't promise that we will never suffer shame in the eyes of the world. He does, however, promise God's salvation and rich blessings from Heaven. In other words, we find honour in the presence of our saviour.

No-one who trusts in God will ever suffer shame before Him.

Suggested prayer: Let's search our hearts. Do you (like me, sometimes) want to look good in front of others? Do we look for honour or praise from people, instead of finding love and acceptance from our saviour? Let's ask God to help us to get our priorities right.

DAY 13

Ecclesiastes

'Meaningless! Meaningless!"
says the Teacher.
Utterly meaningless!
Everything is meaningless' (Eccl 1: 1)

Everyone has days like this. The writer of Ecclesiastes (presumably Solomon?) though, seems to have entered an entire season of it as he takes us on a dark journey questioning the value of virtually everything we hold to or experience in life. Our jobs, careers, all our hard work (v 3); the cycles of nature (v 5 – 7); our history and ancestry (v 11) and new ideas, inventions, creations and the like (v 10).

What's the point? Is it all worth it? 'All things are wearisome; more than one can say' (Eccl 1: 8). Even the pursuit of wisdom and knowledge for pleasure or for their own sakes seems to have left the Teacher uninspired and unsatisfied (v 16 – 18). In fact, he seems to have only gained grief and sorrow.

People have been questioning the meaning of life since the dawn of time, and they still do today. Some find meaning in their careers or vocations, some in their families. Some in a philosophy or religion. Psychologists tell us the feeling that one's life has meaning, or significance can give us positive health outcomes. We feel good when we have a reason to get up in the morning.

But does the Teacher of Ecclesiastes have anything helpful to say? In chapter 2, we are invited to peruse his diary. 'I tried having fun and filling my days with laughter, but what did it ultimately accomplish? I built houses, vineyards, gardens and parks; I became very wealthy and I even had my own choir and personal brothel (yes, really! - v 8)'.

Solomon then denied himself nothing in his pursuit of answers, but still ended up with 'what is my life all about?' His conclusion seems to be that answers are as hard to come by as capturing the wind and holding it in a jar.

Everything is meaningless. Full stop! Until that is, we find a hint of hope at the end of the second chapter.

According to the last three verses of this chapter, it is actually possible to experience satisfaction in our work and pursuits, and we can find genuine joy in the pursuit of wisdom or knowledge – when it is given by God. When God is bought into the equation.

As the Teacher continues his treatise, he develops this. We are encouraged to 'go into the house of God' (5: 1) and listen to Him. God is able to help us to find pleasure in our occupations and possessions (5: 18 – 20). On one hand, there is evil in the world and death awaits us all, but on the other, 'the dust returns to the ground it came from, and the spirit returns to God who gave it' (12: 7). We are eternal beings and that too gives us hope.

We came from God and we can find a relationship with Him both now and in eternity. God can grant us the satisfaction of meaning in the things we do while on planet Earth. Then we will return to Him for an even better and meaningful life. 'He has put eternity into man's heart' (3: 11). The best is yet to come.

Suggested prayer: Thank God for the hope we have in Jesus. Life today has deep meaning when we live it in relationship with Him. And He promises life to come in eternity. Take this moment to re-commit your life to Him; ask Him to show how to live your life, to do the things He has called you to do.

DAY 14

Possessing the Possessions

In Ephesians 1: 15 - 19, Paul writes the following to Christians in churches in and around Ephesus:

'…ever since I heard about your faith in the Lord Jesus and your love for all God's people, I have not stopped giving thanks for you, remembering you in my prayers. I keep asking that the God of our Lord Jesus Christ, the glorious Father, may give you the Spirit of wisdom and revelation, so that you may know Him better. I pray that the eyes of your heart may be enlightened in order that you may know the hope to which he has called you, the riches of his glorious inheritance in his holy people, and his incomparably great power for us who believe'.

As we can see, about half-way through this discourse, Paul prays that the Ephesians' hearts will be enlightened to *know* something – actually three things, and he is very specific. He wants the believers to know three truths, not just assenting to them theologically. Paul passionately petitions God for revelation to occur in the Ephesians' souls and he wants them to live in the good of the things God has given them. He wants them to consciously possess what they received on the day of their salvation. In other words, he wants them to possess their possessions.

The first is Hope. The way this word is used in popular culture is different to way it is used in Scripture. Hope, as defined by Paul in his letters is not subjective; it is not dependent on emotions, but it is a certain knowledge of truths relating to our newfound status in God. God chose us; our sins have been taken away; the Holy Spirit has been given to us; we are 'in Christ' and raised up with him in the heavenly realms (Eph 2: 6). We have a future in Him, throughout the rest of our earthly lives and into eternity. Paul is saying, 'I am praying that you might know that'.

He also prays that the Ephesians will know their Inheritance. The word, 'Grace' comes to mind here – the infinite blessings and promises of God freely given to His own, undeserved, yet poured out in abundance upon His children.

The story of Ira Yates is well-known, the Texan rancher and farmer in the early 20th century, struggling to make ends meet during the American Depression until oil was discovered on his land. Yates had been living as a pauper on land that would make him a millionaire. Paul is praying that the Ephesians will know the rich reserves of Heaven's resources – all the blessings and promises available to them by faith.

And finally, Power. The same divine power that raised Jesus from the dead and seated Him on His royal throne is available to us for the works God has called us to do. God doesn't send us into any situation without first equipping us with the tools we need and the power to carry out the work.

Suggested prayer: Let's pray for ourselves and for those in our care that we might know these things too – our hope in Him, our inheritance and His power. Let's pray that we might know them in our heads, deeply in our hearts and experientially in our daily lives.

DAY 15

God Our Refuge

Many passages of Scripture (particularly the Psalms) describe God as a refuge – a place of safety and protection for the righteous. However, if we are reading the Bible from Genesis to Revelation, or even through a purely historical timeframe, it is a city, or rather cities, that are first described as places of refuge.

In a culture framed by the Lord's instructions to take, 'fracture for fracture, eye for eye, tooth for tooth; whatever injury he has given a person shall be given to him' (Lev 24: 20), provision was needed to shield those who accidentally harmed another, particularly if death had occurred. So, God instructed the Israelites to build cities where someone (a 'manslayer') might run and be guaranteed protection until a fair trial took place.

There were to be six cities altogether and they would belong to the Levites. The Levites were the tribe who served God in the tabernacle, the place of God's presence. They received the sacrifices from the people and offered them up to God. The one seeking safe haven would live among them, but they could not stray from the city boundary, otherwise they would no longer be protected.

The Lord provided a home and food for the Levite and so, also the one seeking sanctuary. For the one taking flight, there was the opportunity to stop at a place of peace and find shelter among the people who served the Lord.

What a wonderful picture of God as our refuge, a place where we stop running and a place of peace, where God's people dwell. Here is a place of divine provision, where fear is no longer the narrative –The psalmist tells us that 'God is our refuge and strength, an ever-present help in trouble. Therefore, I will not fear…' (Ps 46: 1 – 2a).

God's refuge is a place of His presence, where He loves us and wraps His arms around us – 'He is a shield for all who take refuge in Him' (Ps 18: 30).

Here the weary traveler not only rests in God, but he/she also experiences His blessings – 'taste and see that the Lord is good; blessed is the (one) who takes refuge in Him (Ps 34: 8).

When we choose The Lord as our refuge, we can stand our ground against spiritual attack, because the Lord is on His heavenly throne (Ps 11: 4) – 'In the Lord, I take refuge. How then can you say to me: "Flee like a bird to your mountain."' (Ps 11: 1)

Just as the manslayer decides to run to the city of refuge, we too can take intentional steps towards God's spiritual haven. 'I will take refuge in the shadow of your wings,' says the psalmist in 57: 1, a place where 'I can always go' (71: 3).

Why would we put our hope in anything else? 'It is better to take refuge in the Lord than to trust in humans' (Ps 118: 8).

Suggested prayer: Lord, you are my refuge, my place of safety and protection. Thank you that you wrap me in your arms. There is no fear in you, only peace. Lord, I declare that I trust you; I rest under the shadow of your wings. Amen.

DAY 16

The Most Beautiful Thing I have ever Seen

Something struck me in the book of Exodus the other day.

For two days shy of six weeks, Moses had been alone on a mountain in the very presence of God. During that time, he received detailed instructions for the building of a tabernacle, where sacrifice and offerings would become the norm and where the people would meet with God.

The walls, furniture and utensils would be made from materials given freely by the Israelite community, from young and old, from everyone 'whose heart moved him' (Ex 25: 1). The donations were so generous that Moses was eventually forced to call for a stop to the giving (Ex 36: 6).

It was one particular aspect of God's instructions to Moses that fascinated me – in chapter 28: the design of the priests clothing, their uniform for carrying out their duties. Verse two (and 40) outlines God's purpose for Aaron and his sons to wear special garments – 'for glory and for beauty.' The reason they had specific clothes to wear was for glory and beauty.

Nearly every other item to be manufactured for the tabernacle had a clear function. The alter was made to burn the sacrifices, the lampstand to light the room and the ark to contain the 10 commandments. What were the priests' clothes for? Glory and beauty.

Today, God requires no tabernacle to meet with His people. Jesus' death on the cross has provided a way for us come into His presence through a simple prayer of repentance and faith. Collectively we become building blocks of a new holy place – the church. The New Testament is clear: every time we gather together in His name, God is there too.

So, what are churches for? Why do they exist? I'm sure, between us, we could come up with a sizable list of functions, from preaching and teaching to ministering to the poor, to sharing the Gospel and so on, but I wonder how many would say, 'churches exist for glory and beauty'?

The church is also described as a bride, so, what is usually said of a bride as she walks down the aisle towards her husband-to-be? Easy - She is beautiful!

I recently, and quite suddenly, saw all of this with new eyes as I was thinking about the purpose of the church today in our modern world. We congregate in churches and homes and we do the work of serving and building. We carry out the functions of church, but it struck me that we are also called to be beautiful – to radiate the beauty that God gives us, shining in the world, boldly declaring what He has done, reigning in life as sons and daughters of God, doing His work, and revealing His glory. We were created to be beautiful.

No wonder Jesus said, 'let your light shine before others, that they may see your good deeds and glorify your Father in heaven' (Matt 5: 16). When we serve God with all of our hearts, according to His mighty plans and purposes, we not only fulfill the functions of church, but we also display glory and beauty too.

One day we will see the Church comprising every tribe and nation surrounding the throne of the lamb and many, I'm sure, will spontaneously fall to their knees and declare, 'this is the most beautiful thing I have ever seen'.

Imagine us serving well and building well today, with pure hearts and true to His plans. Then, maybe a new generation will discover Jesus and, with tears of joy, say of His Church, 'this is the most beautiful thing I have ever seen.'

Suggested prayer: Pray for the church around the world, in your nation and, if you have one, your own church. Pray that God's glory and beauty be displayed in all we do, in the words we speak and in the love that we show to a dying world.

DAY 17

Putting on the Right Clothes

The forecast was clear: it was going to be a sweltering day. No clouds in the sky. Get the sunscreen out. Wear a hat and sunglasses.

Unfortunately, I was scheduled to attend a meeting where shorts wouldn't cut it. It would need to be long pants/trousers, smart shoes and an ironed shirt for the occasion. I felt sweaty already. Later, when my wife and I finished our meeting, we jumped in the car as soon as we could.

There were items we needed to buy from a hardware store on the way home, so we parked the car and walked in. It felt even hotter inside the warehouse despite the air conditioning and I couldn't wait to get home, throw my shirt off and change my clothes.

I remember another time several years prior, visiting London in the UK in the middle of winter and feeling the biting cold wind through a very unsuitable, thin rain-jacket.

In both of these scenarios, I was wearing the wrong clothes.

Paul talks about taking off some garments and putting on others in his letter to the Colossians (3: 5 – 14). He reminds them that they have 'taken off' their old selves – who they were and what they did before knowing Christ (v 9, see also 2: 11). Instead, they have 'put on the new self', a spiritual piece of clothing that enjoys continual renewal as their knowledge of God grows (v 10).

Embracing this new coat in their daily lives, the Colossians can also 'clothe themselves' with Christ's compassion, kindness, humility, gentleness and patience (v 12). Dressed from the right wardrobe – the daily provision of God's grace through prayer and His Word - they have the power to bear with one another and forgive each other. They can 'put on' love (v 14) because that coat sits on a hanger, already paid for and ready for use.

It seems to me in this passage that God is telling us (through Paul) to put on what He has already given us. We have a whole new wardrobe of spiritual blessings at no cost to us. The freedom to live a new life was paid for on the cross, but unless we take hold of them, unless we take steps to put them on, like pushing our arms into the sleeves of a new jacket, they will be like undiscovered gifts, hanging in a closet with the door shut.

Paul doesn't want to see anyone in his churches dressed inappropriately or hanging on to an old shirt that needs to be burned. He wants these followers of Christ to fully embrace everything God has for them – free from the soiled clothes of sin and selfishness, but clean and beautiful in the garments of our salvation. Perhaps God wants the same for us.

God has given us a stunning new outfit – a new life in Christ Jesus. Do we put it on, proudly, every day or do we think about rummaging around for some of our old, soiled clothes?

Perhaps it is time to do some throwing out?

Suggested prayer: Lord, thank you for the price you paid on the cross. You surrendered your life to a cruel death that we might be forgiven and set free from the things we have done wrong. I can now take off my old clothes of sin and proudly wear a new outfit of your freedom and righteousness. Amen

DAY 18

Following Jesus

Right at the beginning of Jesus' ministry, we find Him inviting a handful of fishermen to be His disciples. He asks them to 'Come, follow me!' (Mark 1: 17). '…and I will send you out to fish for people'. They must have wondered what he meant.

Straight after this, Mark tells us that Jesus was preaching with authority, He was casting out demons and He was healing the sick.

Sometime later in chapter six, Jesus sent His 12 disciples out to the nearby towns and villages. Guess what he was asking them to do: preach repentance (Mark 6: 12) and preach the Kingdom (Matt 10: 7), deliver people from evil spirits and heal the sick (Matt 10: 1). Luke also records a time when the disciples plus many others (72 in total) were sent out to do the same.

Many students in 1st century Palestine sought out the Rabbis they wished to follow. Jesus took the initiative and chose these fishermen. A *talmidim* (disciple) of a conventional Rabbi would have demonstrated an impressive knowledge of the Old Testament law, and he would have been as eager as his master to enforce the Pharisees oral law. Jesus often spoke against the Pharisees' ways to His disciples. The Jewish rabbis stressed separation from non-Jews and those that were unclean. Jesus taught His disciples that loving our neighbours is as important as loving God.

Jesus was no ordinary Rabbi. His priorities were very different to those of His contemporaries and following Him was not like following other rabbis.

After the resurrection, Jesus instructed His disciples to continue doing the same three things – preach, deliver people from evil spirits and lay hands on the sick - and there is a strong inference that the command is for us too – 'for those who believe' (Mark 16: 17).

When I ask myself, the question, 'what does it mean to follow Jesus?', I find I can't move away from His unconventional (at the time) example: preach repentance and the things of the Kingdom, deliver people from evil and heal the sick.

So, what does that look like, today in the 21st century?

We may not all feel that we are preachers, but we probably have a story of God's love and grace in our hearts. How might we share it with those around us? There has never been a time in history with such ease of communication. How might God want us to use our technology to further His Kingdom?

We may or may not have consciously experienced the kingdom of darkness in the form of evil spirits but evil thrives around us, sometimes overwhelmingly so where do we start? Someone once said that the place you fight cruelty is where you find it, just as the place you give help is where you see it is needed.

Psychologists will tell us that there is a link between healing and physical touch. Apparently, it is well-known that there are health benefits associated with a hug or a simple holding of a person's hand during a time of illness or distress. Two wonders may occur through the touch of a hand – the power of the Holy Spirit to heal and the miracle of God's love to the soul.

You don't have to look far to see the worlds of darkness, cruelty and sickness. They are on our doorsteps. Let's follow Jesus into those worlds as preachers, deliverers and healers.

Suggested prayer: Pray for opportunities to share the story of Jesus with others. Then expect opportunities to come your way. Where do you see evil or injustice in the world? Pray for ways to shine His light into the darkness. Pray that God might use you to bring His healing to others, either through prayer or through a simple touch or hug.

DAY 19

Forgiveness

That person really hurt me Lord, why should I forgive them?

'Forgive us our sins, as we have forgiven those who sin against us' (Matt 6: 12 NLT).

'If you forgive those who sin against you, your heavenly Father will forgive you. But if you refuse to forgive others, your Father will not forgive your sins' (Matt 6: 14).

That seems a bit harsh! God knows I haven't done the things they've done.

'…all have sinned and fall short of the glory of God' (Rom 3: 23).

'…who can discern their own errors? Forgive my hidden faults' (Ps 19: 12).

OK, I can forgive them once; maybe twice, I could stretch to three times, but not any more than that!

Peter came to Jesus and asked, 'Lord, how many times shall I forgive my brother or sister who sins against me? Up to seven times?' Jesus answered, 'I tell you, not seven times, but seventy times seven times' (Matt 18: 21 – 22).

Lord, you don't know what I've been through, it's too hard.

'Pilate took Jesus and had him flogged. The soldiers twisted together a crown of thorns and put it on His head. They clothed him in a purple robe and went up to him again and again, saying, "Hail, king of the Jews!" And they slapped him in the face' (John 19: 1 – 3).

'When they came to the place called the Skull, they crucified him there, along with the criminals—one on His right, the other on His left. Jesus said, "Father, forgive them, for they do not know what they are doing"' (Luke 23: 33 – 34).

'Bear with each other and forgive one another if any of you has a grievance against someone. Forgive as the Lord forgave you' (Col 3: 13).

I know God is a God of second chances, but I don't believe He'll forgive everything. I don't even forgive myself for some of the things I have done.

'If we confess our sins, he is faithful and just and will forgive us our sins and purify us from all unrighteousness' (1 John 1: 9)

I must admit, it would be so good to be released of this heavy burden of guilt.

'Blessed are those whose transgressions are forgiven; whose sins are covered.
Blessed is the one whose sin the Lord will never count against them' (Rom 4: 7 – 8)

Then Jesus said, 'Come to me, all of you who are weary and carry heavy burdens, and I will give you rest. Take my yoke upon you. Let me teach you, because I am humble and gentle at heart, and you will find rest for your souls. For my yoke is easy to bear, and the burden I give you is light' (Matt 11: 28 – 30 NLT)

Suggested prayer: Lord, thank you that you are a forgiving God. When I think of all the things I have done, in thought, word and deed that hurt you and others, I am amazed that you would go to the cross for me. Please wash me clean of my sin and help me to extend the same mercy to others who have wronged me. In Jesus' name, Amen.

DAY 20

The Next Step

I first came across Psalm 119: 105 as a new Christian through a song recorded by Amy Grant back in 1984. Some of the lyrics I remember are:

When I feel afraid
Think I've lost my way
Still you're there right beside me
And nothing will I fear
As long as you are near
Please be near me to the end

Thy Word is a lamp unto my feet and a light unto my path
Songwriters: Amy Lee Grant / Michael Whitaker Smith
© 1984 Curb Word Music (Admin. by CopyCare Pacific Pty. Ltd.) Meadowgreen Music Company

With 176 verses, Psalm 119 is the longest Psalm in the Bible. Commonly known as the 'Everest of the Psalter', it is roughly the same length as the book of Philippians.

It is a celebration of God's commands. Beautifully constructed around the Hebrew alphabet, we are reminded of the countless blessings that flow into our lives when His Word and our hearts combine. God's law brings comfort (v 52), wisdom (v 98), understanding (v 30) and joy (v 111).

About two-thirds of the way through, the psalmist seems to pause for a moment, and then utters the words that have become known as verse 105:

'Your word is a lamp to my feet and a light for my path.'

I imagine a traveler passing through a thick, dark forest in the middle of the night. With one hand she grips the lapels of her coat tightly against her chin to shield her from the cold, and with the other hand she holds a lantern.

The warm glow of light emitted from the lamp is enough to see what is directly in front of her and to safely take the next step, but she can see no further. She only knows the direction, the path she must go and where to place her feet right now.

I have sometimes found myself praying, 'Lord, could you give me the next five years in detail?' I want to know how things are going to work out, whether the work I am putting in is going to be worth it. But when I read this verse, I think God is reminding me that He is faithful to grant me enough light for just the next step. And that is sufficient for now.

The idea of going on a journey or walking along a path is a recurrent theme in this psalm and throughout Scripture. The author deeply desires to avoid the wrong path, but he finds delight (v 35) and freedom to live a pure life on the right path centred on God's Word.

Our path through life may sometimes feel like we are walking though a cold, dark and confusing forest, but God's Spirit is in us and His Word never leaves us. As we learn to trust the warm glow of His commands and decrees, responding with simple baby steps, one after the other, we eventually find the clearing and the light of day.

And along the way, we can celebrate His Word with a simple song in our hearts: *Thy Word is a lamp unto my feet and a light unto my path.*

Suggested prayer: Lord, your Word is all I need. Your promises, wisdom, guidance and encouragement are all found within the pages of Scripture. Lord, I don't ask you for more details than I can handle about the future, but I trust you for enough light to take the next step forward. Amen.

DAY 21

The Place of Highest Authority

The famous story of Jesus calming a storm is an intriguing one. First, experienced, and hardened fishermen were afraid of wind and waves – it must have been one heck of a storm! Second because Jesus, rather than understanding this, actually rebukes the disciples for their lack of faith (Mark 6: 35 – 41).

But perhaps Jesus had a point.

Up 'til then, His disciples had heard a voice from heaven announcing Him to be God's son and they had seen Him do miracle after miracle including a paralytic walking, a man with leprosy being completely healed and demons cast out with a word of command. They heard evil spirits declaring Jesus to be the 'Holy one of God' (Mark 1: 24) and they heard Jesus forgiving sins, re-writing the rules of the sabbath and teaching in such a profound new way that He left his audiences stunned and 'amazed' (Mark 1: 22).

Maybe the disciples just forgot who was in the boat with them!

And perhaps that is the moral of the story. When storms hit, how easy is it to take our eyes off the One who created them and, by the way, who is right next to us! For many of us, it doesn't seem to take much to feel afraid, overwhelmed and helpless, but ask yourself: 'do I need to?' Jesus started the journey with us, He knows where He is going, He knows where He is taking us, and He hasn't left us.

The storms that hit us can be forces we are expecting, or they can creep up from behind unannounced. They can occur through circumstances, through people or through both. They can come at us from things that we see, or they can slowly grow within. Perhaps those are the deadliest ones, the ones that swirl around inside us and try to steal our peace. How do we fight them?

Jesus commanded the wind and waves to be quiet and still. He used His authority to calm the tempest. Now, here's the thing: Did you know that you and I have that same authority? In Ephesians 2: 6, Paul describes our spiritual status as 'raised up with Christ and seated with him in the heavenly realms.' That folk is the place of highest authority.

We may not be able to control every external influence, but when it comes to the storms that rage within, maybe we can use some of that authority to do some commanding. Look at the way David spoke to his heart in Psalm 42: 11:

> 'Why, my soul, are you downcast?
> Why so disturbed within me?
> Put your hope in God'.

Have you done any commanding lately?

It might be time to start telling your soul to 'be quiet and still'; to speak to your heart: 'Come on heart, put your hope in God!', and then remember who you are positioned next to. You are in the throne room of the king – in Christ – the place of highest authority.

Suggested prayer: Do you feel you are facing a storm at the moment? Do you sometimes think that parts of your life are like a sinking boat? Thank Jesus for being in the boat with you. Speak to your soul – command it to put its trust in the One who can bring peace and calm to any situation.

DAY 22

Family

I think most people in this world would agree with Dominic Toretto when he said, 'The most important thing in your life will always be family' (*Fast and Furious*)

God created family, of course. We first meet the idea of marriage when God found a partner for Adam, Eve, and it was meant to be an inseparable bond. Sadly, sin stained the world and we have lived in a broken world ever since. People mess up, and marriages become less than perfect. Or break up completely.

However, in Jesus, there is always grace and forgiveness. New beginnings. God's heart has always been to join people in families and to see family life flourish. In this context, children are a gift and a blessing. But also, a responsibility.

Does God have a *purpose* in creating families? Emphatically, Yes! Let me suggest three ways.

First, families are the vehicle God has chosen to pass on His truth and stories to the next generation. 'These commandments that I give you today are to be on your hearts. Impress them on your children. Talk about them when you sit at home and when you walk along the road, when you lie down and when you get up' (Deut 6: 6 – 7). How will the next generation know about God unless they are told – unless they are taught? And, unless it is modeled for them.

Similarly, families were designed to reveal God's love and truth to a dying world. The way we do family will speak to those around us, in our streets and in our communities. 'A new command I give you: Love one another. As I have loved you, so you must love one another. By this everyone will know that you are my disciples, if you love one another' (John 13: 34 – 35)

Third, families are a training ground to equip the next generation to serve

God. We may have young children at home, or we may see nieces or nephews or cousins or grandchildren. If they are not yet adults, they are on loan to us for a season, and that season will pass quickly! In that short time, how are we teaching them to serve the Lord? How are we equipping them to be servants that bless those around them?

For example, a lot of people in today's world choose churches that have a flourishing Sunday school or a great youth program. They look for what will serve their children best. Here's an alternative idea: How about looking for a church that needs help? How about choosing a church where the whole family can learn to serve? How about we teach our children to put God first by joining a church family where they can begin to use their gifts to meet a need there?

As much as I love the *Fast and Furious* movies, I think Dominic Toretto was wrong. The most important thing isn't family; it's that as a family we learn to love God and serve those around us.

Suggested prayer: Think about your family or those in your care. How might you lead or show by example an attitude of serving others. Pray for the generations younger than you – that they might know Christ and be inspired by others to serve Him and put Him first.

DAY 23

The Pharisee Within

People have swallowed the weirdest things.

We all expect young children to put small objects in their mouths (and we try to stop them, of course), but then there are the adults.

One man in Croatia was found to have a lighter in his stomach. He had intentionally swallowed it whilst at a police station because it contained a small quantity of drugs and incriminating evidence against him.

Another, a 29-year-old in Ireland, swallowed a small cell phone and then there was the story of the 18-year-old who was trying to induce vomiting with a toothbrush and, well, you can guess the rest!

Some things are not meant to be inside us.

Have you ever wondered why are there so many accounts in the gospels about the Pharisees and about their rules and Jesus' confrontations with them? So serious were those conversations that Jesus felt the need to say to His disciples, 'Be on your guard against the yeast (the teaching) of the Pharisees and Sadducees' (Matt 16: 6). We know that 'All scripture is God-breathed and is useful for teaching, rebuking, correcting, and training in righteousness' (2 Tim 3: 16), so why do we read so many stories about these guys? Surely, they don't exist today!

I was talking with a friend a while back. I had gently challenged him about a particular attitude he was displaying when he asked, 'Do you think I am a Pharisee?' Taken aback, I said 'no, but I think there may be a hidden Pharisee in all of us.' That may seem a bit of a stretch, but for me if I am honest, I know there is one in me. I try to hide him, but he is definitely in there. What is he up to? Well, like a virus, he is silently trying to spread his influence. So, in what ways does he try to influence?

Let's try something different. Let me invite you to participate in the 'Do I have the Pharisee virus?' test. Are you ready?

- How hard do you work to look good on the outside? I am not talking about a new haircut to make you even more beautiful; I am talking about your secret desire that everyone you meet will believe that you are a good person? In other words, do you seek the praise of others more than the praise of God?

- How easy is it for you to apologise? Or are you rarely in the wrong? Do you recognise moments when you fall short of God's best or you or do find it hard to admit a fault?

- When you meet someone who lives, let's say, a 'colourful life' – do you compare yourself to them? Do you think you are better? When was the last time you prayed, 'have mercy on me, Lord, a sinner'?

So, how did you get on? Did you think you tested positive or negative for the Pharisee virus?

It is so easy to read the Gospels and pass judgment on the Pharisees of Jesus' day, but perhaps it takes some humility and courage to recognise that, sometimes, there may be a little Pharisee inside us too. Let's make an agreement together: our hearts belong to God; the Pharisee has no place there!

Suggested prayer: Ask God to show you any Pharisee traits that hide in your heart. Name each one of them and repent of them. Then ask God to replace them with His love, mercy, humility, grace and kindness.

DAY 24

Set Apart

I know it's obvious, but I believe there is a fundamental difference between dogs and cats.

They are both pets, they can be adoringly cute (and they can be really annoying), but there is one thing that separates them, apart from anatomy, and apart the fact that one goes 'meow' while the other goes 'woof?'

It is all to do with displays of affection.

Take my two cats for example. Reho (the white one) and Toosy (the black evil one, should have called him 'Vader') will occasionally act as if they like me. Reho will donate large wads of fur as he rubs himself against my leg, purring away as if to say, 'I love you; you are so wonderful…' etc. Toosy will give a little chirp of delight whenever I enter the room as if to call out, 'It is SO good to see you, please stay a while'.

I don't believe a word of it!

They want me for what they can get out of me – food, an extra bit of attention, you name it.

On the other hand, dog owners will tell me how excited their canine friends are when they come home, barking and licking with excitement. They are not after any treats, they just love being with their human.

Too simplistic? Your pet may or may not fit that mould exactly, but I was thinking about this as I read Acts 13: 2 recently. The church in Antioch were worshipping, fasting and praying and the Holy Spirit spoke (presumably through one of the prophets mentioned in verse 1) these words, 'Set apart for me Barnabas and Saul for the work to which I have called them. *Set apart*. There is a conscious decision here, not least in the hearts of Barnabas and Saul, to something deeper than just attending a prayer meeting. Something deeper that just doing church. They are to be set apart.

If I am honest, there are times when I treat God in the same way that I believe my cats are treating me. I am at home in God's house like Toosy and Reho are in mine. I belong to God, like my cats belong to me, but I sometimes worship and pray to God because I want something from Him. It might be peace, wisdom, guidance, a miracle, and God graciously keeps His Word and gives me those things, but how often do I just come to Him to enjoy a moment with Him? To say thank you. To say, 'I love you' and mean it.

There are some lovely descriptions of Barnabas in earlier chapters of Acts. He was a 'good man, full of the Holy Spirit and faith' (Acts 11: 24) and he saw the grace of God in others (v 23). You get the impression that he was a 'man after God's own heart' like David was centuries before him.

I imagine Barnabas to be already 'set apart' for God even before that important prayer meeting in Acts 13 – set apart in his heart. He didn't just go to church because that's what he did (or because he had to – he was the pastor!), I bet he didn't just present a list of requests every time he prayed. You get the impression that Barnabas simply loved God – no strings attached!

I think the world is in desperate need for more people like Barnabas.

Suggested prayer: Spend some time with the Lord in prayer. If you have things to ask him, for yourself or for another, put those to one side and come back to them later. Make it your priority today to just 'be' in His presence. Express your love, your gratitude, repent if you need to. Worship Him. Don't be afraid of silence. Listen to the gentle whispers of His Spirit.

DAY 25

Gazing on the Beauty of the Lord

'One thing I ask from the Lord,
this only do I seek:
that I may dwell in the house of the Lord
all the days of my life,
to gaze on the beauty of the Lord
and to seek him in his temple.' (Ps 27: 4)

I think I understand what 'seeking' means – an intentional act of continually approaching God in prayer and worship, asking for help, guidance, revelation etc. But what about gazing upon His beauty? How do we gaze upon the beauty of the invisible God (Col 1: 15)?

I sat by the window at the front of my house and looked out. The cordylines on the other side of the glass paraded their magnificent leaves. I refocused my eyes to bushland on the other side of the road with its plethora of shapes and hues of brown and green. The sun had risen an hour before and shafts of light were beginning to break through the gaps between branches and trees.

A fly distracted me, and I suppressed the impulse to reach for the fly spray after I noticed the intricate designs on his wings. The sun's rays reached the inside of my room and I felt their warmth on my legs. I realised the wind was picking up as branches and leaves in near and far view danced together, and I became aware that the voices of nature had been singing all along.

A car drove by. I started to marvel about how God has gifted us with the ability to imagine, design and create complex things. A dog took its owner for a walk and made me smile; the clouds synchronised to form another masterpiece in the sky.

In just a few minutes, God had been with me in the sights and the sounds, in the warmth of the sun and in my imagination. Is this what it means to gaze upon the beauty of the Lord?

I started to talk to Him. I told Him what I liked in the scene in front of me, and I was thankful for the beauty in the details. I started to picture myself sitting in His presence – at peace, in the place of healing and restoration, where the light is pure, penetrating everything and yet warm with love. I was like a child, sitting on the floor, an arm's reach from his father, happy and content.

I don't know if any of this held any similarities to David's thoughts as he imagined gazing on the beauty of the Lord in Psalm 27, but one thing was certain: Like David, the more I stopped to ponder God's love and greatness, the more I wanted to be there, the more I wanted to put down roots and dwell there, all the days of my life.

Maybe this is why David, at the end of the psalm, can declare, boldly 'I remain confident of this: I will see the goodness of the Lord in the land of the living' (Ps 27: 13).

Suggested prayer: Lord, help me to stop each day long enough to sit at your feet and ponder your love and greatness. I don't want to be so busy that I miss the many signs of your grace all around me. Please open up my ears, eyes and senses to your daily presence. Amen.

DAY 26

Wisdom and Knowledge

Many of us are fascinated by stories of buried treasure. In 2007, Jeff Bidelman knocked down a wall in an abandoned home. He had noticed a hole in the wall and as he started enlarging it, coins flooded out. Eventually he recovered hundreds of valuable pieces worth over $100,000.

But not all treasure is discovered so easily. In the well-known reality TV show, *The Curse of Oak Island*, seven seasons to 2020 chronicle the, sometimes, painfully slow progress of Rick and Marty Lagina as they try to uncover the buried secrets of the island. Some things require a lot of effort and a lot of patience.

As we read Paul's letter to the Colossian church, we catch a glimpse of his struggles and sheer hard work, as he seeks to help believers in Jesus to grow in their new-found faith: 'Him we proclaim, warning everyone and teaching everyone with all wisdom, that we may present everyone mature in Christ. For this I toil, struggling with all his energy that he powerfully works within me' (Col 1: 28 – 29 ESV).

He wants them to discover treasure.

'My goal is that they may be encouraged in heart and united in love, so that they may have the full riches of complete understanding, in order that they may know the mystery of God, namely, Christ' (Col 2: 2). Riches. Mystery. The end-goal is Christ, 'in whom are hidden all the treasures of wisdom and knowledge' (v 3).

I like that. There are depths to knowing Jesus that we haven't even started to explore. There are treasures. According to this, if we really want to tap into the deep reservoirs of God, the journey starts (and continues) by getting to know His Son. Divine wisdom and infinite knowledge are found in Christ, but it is not all unearthed in a moment. It is a life-long adventure. It's like an ongoing quest to find a buried trove of riches.

In our own Christian lives, we can often feel like explorers. I know that is certainly true for me. The ancient texts of Scripture guide us along paths and they sometimes reveal gold nuggets of truth at just the right moment. At other times, circumstances seem to push hard against us, and the trek can feel like we are on rugged, tough terrain. It can be a struggle to stay true to the goal of knowing Christ. It is not always easy to plumb the depths of His wisdom and knowledge.

Paul has good advice for such believers, prescribing it all like medicine taken daily, 'and now, just as you accepted Christ Jesus as your Lord, you must continue to follow him. Let your *roots grow down* into him, and let your *lives be built* on him. Then your faith will grow strong in the truth you were taught, and you will overflow with thankfulness' (Col 2: 6 – 7 NLT).

Put down your roots in Him and build every part of your life on Him. Do you want a deeper relationship with Christ? Do you want to discover more of His treasures of wisdom and knowledge? Then root and build your life on Him – every part of it.

Suggested prayer: Try to see your journey with Jesus as a lifelong adventure, searching for treasures as we grow in wisdom and knowledge. Day in and day out. Year in and year out. Pray that you will develop perseverance during the tough seasons. Ask Him to help you to dig deeper into Him, that your relationship with Him might keep growing, and growing.

DAY 27

Treasures

'Do not store up for yourselves treasures on earth, where moths and vermin destroy, and where thieves break in and steal. But store up for yourselves treasures in heaven, where moths and vermin do not destroy, and where thieves do not break in and steal. For where your treasure is, there your heart will be also' (Matt 6: 19 – 21).

What is your treasure?

We treasure a lot of things don't we and one might argue they are not necessarily 'wrong' things. Our family can often be our greatest blessing and who can put a price on the value of good friends ("There is a friend who sticks closer than a brother" Prov 18: 24)? We are also grateful for good health, work, and happy memories.

There are some things that we *know* are wrong to treasure, for example, the accumulation of wealth and possessions for their own sake, or ambitions for my own ego's sake. These are what we might call treasures on Earth. But what about those other 'good' things – are they treasures on Earth or heaven?

Perhaps that is asking wrong question. Sometimes I pray, 'Lord I want you to be Lord of my life, but it's a struggle.' Why? Because my heart is often in other things.

So, maybe it comes down to a different question: how much are we treasuring God? How much are we treasuring His kingdom coming; His name being lifted high; the gospel being shared in the lives of those around us? How much are we treasuring our personal relationship with Him; His will being outworked in our lives? How much do we want to value those things above all else?

A few verses later, Jesus reminds His hearers of our Father in Heaven's care of all living things. If He does that for the birds and lilies, then he will provide for us too.

'So,' says Jesus, 'don't stress yourself worrying about those things, instead put your energy into building the Kingdom of God with me' (Matt 6: 25 – 33)

Which brings us back to my question, how much am I treasuring God? If I am treasuring God, that must mean that I am seeking first His kingdom, right? And then what does He promise? He promises to look after all those other things – food, clothing, the things we worry about.

Then there is a curious passage in Matt 7: 13 – 14: 'Enter through the narrow gate. For wide is the gate and broad is the road that leads to destruction, and many enter through it. But small is the gate and narrow the road that leads to life, and only a few find it'.

I used to think that this was about people becoming Christians and not pursuing other religions. But maybe it is to do with doing life. 'Narrow' is often seen as a negative word. It has negative connotations. We can be narrow-minded or have a narrow point of view. But what if Jesus had more in mind the ability to be focused?

A person that is focused can run a marathon, climb a mountain, or reach a high level of musical skill. The pursuit of those activities is of huge importance to them. So, maybe a person who is focused on putting the Kingdom of God first, trusting Him to look after all those other things, will be a person who treasures God above everything else.

And according to Jesus, that road leads to *life*. After all, Jesus did promise, 'I have come that you have life; and life to the full' (John 10: 10).

Suggested prayer: Lord, I want to experience a life lived to the full, but I know that means treasuring you above all things. And trusting you for everything else. Lord, help me to put the Kingdom of God first and to be focused on your priorities. Amen.

DAY 28

Fruitfulness

I want my life to mean something.

'Produce fruit in keeping with repentance, and do not begin to say to yourselves, We have Abraham as our father. For I tell you that out of these stones God can raise up children for Abraham.' (Luke 3: 8)

Repentance? What are you saying?

'By their fruit you will recognize them. Do people pick grapes from thorn bushes, or figs from thistles? Likewise, every good tree bears good fruit, but a bad tree bears bad fruit. A good tree cannot bear bad fruit, and a bad tree cannot bear good fruit.' (Matt 7: 16 – 18)

Are you saying I'm bad fruit?

'And Peter said to them, "Repent and be baptized every one of you in the name of Jesus Christ for the forgiveness of your sins, and you will receive the gift of the Holy Spirit. For the promise is for you and for your children and for all who are far off, everyone whom the Lord our God calls to himself."' (Acts 2: 38 – 39)

And I will bear good fruit if I receive the Holy Spirit?

'The fruit of the Spirit is love, joy, peace, patience, kindness, goodness, faithfulness, gentleness, self-control.' (Gal 5: 22)

....

'This is my prayer: that your love may abound more and more in knowledge and depth of insight, so that you may be able to discern what is best and may be pure and blameless for the day of Christ, filled with the fruit of righteousness that comes through Jesus Christ—to the glory and praise of God.' (Phil 1: 9 – 11)

If I am understanding you right – God wants me to grow in knowledge, depth of insight, discernment, purity and righteous living. My life will mean something, then, right? I will be fruitful?

'This is to my Father's glory, that you bear much fruit, showing yourselves to be my disciples.' (John 15: 8)

Is there anything else I need to do?

'Let us continually offer to God a sacrifice of praise—the fruit of lips that openly profess his name.' (Heb 13: 15)

'We have not stopped praying for you. We continually ask God to fill you with the knowledge of his will through all the wisdom and understanding that the Spirit gives, so that you may live a life worthy of the Lord and please him in every way: bearing fruit in every good work, growing in the knowledge of God.' (Col 1: 9 – 10)

That sounds like a lot; will God help me?

'I am the vine; you are the branches. If you remain in me and I in you, you will bear much fruit; apart from me you can do nothing.' (John 15: 5)

I want my life to have meaning. What does a fruitful life actually look like?

'Live as children of light for the fruit of the light consists in all goodness, righteousness and truth.' (Eph 5: 9)

Suggested prayer: Lord, I want my life to consist of goodness, your righteousness and truth. I am not going to pray for success in everything I do, because sometimes you mould and shape us through failure, or through setbacks. Rather, I ask that my life be fruitful. Please fill me with the Holy Spirit and grow me in knowledge, depth of insight, discernment, purity and righteous living. Amen.

DAY 29

Eating for the Glory of God

Did you know that God uses food to build the Kingdom of God?

Do I hear a 'Hallelujah'?

One way God teaches us to use food to build His Kingdom is by us sharing what we have with others. The Bible calls it hospitality. Let's consider three ways:

Romans 12: 13 says, 'Share with God's people who are *in need*. Practice hospitality.'

The Bible tells us to love and share what we have with fellow Christians who have little. This follows from the beginning of the chapter when Paul says, 'Therefore, I urge you, brothers and sisters, in view of God's mercy, to offer your bodies as a living sacrifice.' Surely one of the best ways to sacrifice is to give something to bless another!

Who do you know who is doing it tough? – having a difficult time. One meal may not change their situation, but it might remind them of God's love and care for them.

1 Pet 4: 9 reminds us to, 'Love each other deeply… Offer hospitality to *one another* without grumbling. Each of you should use whatever gift you have received to serve others.' The emphasis here is less on those in need and more on 'one another' in the body of Christ. Can I throw you another challenge?

When was the last time you had a guest (from your church) in your home for a meal? And what about that brother or sister, or family who never gets invited anywhere – is God calling you to show them friendship through hospitality?

Lastly, Jesus said, 'And if you greet only your own people, what are you doing more than others? Do not even pagans do that?' (Matt 5: 47)

Perhaps one thing that ought to set us apart from others in the world is that we give a warm hand of welcome to *all* people. One more challenge if I may: Let's welcome those who are not-yet-believers into our homes, too. Let's welcome the lonely, the unloved, the culturally different, those we don't know that well yet.

Jonathan Leeman writes, 'A meal says more than you think.'

If that is true, then what message does an invitation to share a meal give? Let me suggest two things:

- To Christians: we are brothers, we are sisters, we are united in Christ. You are important to God and so you are important to me. You are welcome at my table

- To the not-yet believer: you are welcome at my table because God loves you and He wants a relationship with you.

Suggested prayer: Pray for opportunities to bless people through food. Ask God to show you someone who might value a friend at this time. Has God laid on your heart a person or persons at church who you may not know that well? And ask God for opportunities to reach those who don't yet know him through hospitality.

DAY 30

Watchmen

I wonder how observant you are.

This scenario has played out for me several times: My wife and I will be driving home, and we will be discussing conversations we have had with people earlier in the day. I will say something like, 'that was a really good chat with so-and-so' and she will say, 'I felt there was something wrong. There is something troubling her.'

I hadn't noticed!

In 2 Samuel 18: 24, a watchman for King David climbed on a roof high enough to see beyond the city walls and report on two distant runners coming their way. Another watchman did a similar thing for King Joram in 2 Kings 9: 17. Watchmen trained their eyes to observe what might be approaching the city. They gave an up-to-date news report and sounded a warning if there was the possibility of danger.

Watchmen recognised good news approaching in Isaiah's prophecy (Is 52: 7 – 10), and subsequently lifted up their voices, shouting for joy and proclaiming peace and salvation to the people of God within the city walls

When Ezekiel was called to be a prophet, his God-given role was compared to that of a watchman (Ezek 3: 17), but in this case, he is one who hears. His ears are attuned to the Lord. What God says, Ezekiel must speak out. It therefore makes sense that watchmen must also be people of prayer as in Isaiah 62: 6 – 7, calling on God for the establishment of His purposes.

So, a watchman observes, hears, prays and speaks. He/she watches the world attentively to notice the things God wants them to see and he/she is quiet enough to hear the words the Lord wants them to hear. All of this occurs within a framework of ongoing prayer and when the time is right, they speak out.

I felt the Lord impress upon me recently that to be effective in doing the work He has called me to do, I had to learn to be a watchman.

What does that mean in practice? I think, firstly, it is learning to notice and carefully observe what is going on around me – in this person or that situation. To see the things the Lord wants me to see. Not to just assume things about people, but to seek the kind of discernment that He gives my wife.

When Philip shared the Gospel with the Ethiopian in Acts 8: 26 – 40, the Holy Spirit instructed him to first go near the man, but not to engage straight away. There is a strong implication in the text that Philip needed to observe and listen before doing anything else. After this, it was clear to Philip how he was to proceed, and, as a result, the Ethiopian discovered the good news of Jesus Christ.

Secondly, I think it means to be unhurried in my time with God – hard to do in today's busy world, but essential; and to recognise the gentle whispers of His Spirit.

Of course, the ultimate watchman is the Lord Himself. Psalm 127 reminds us that, 'unless the Lord watches over the city, the watchmen stand guard in vain' (Ps 127: 1b). So, let us learn to be watchmen and watchwomen under the inspiration and guidance of the chief watchman Himself. Let's slow down. Observe, hear, and pray. Then speak and act, as He leads the way.

Suggested prayer. Ask the Lord to give you eyes that can see what He wants you to see. To observe those around you and notice the things He is doing. Ask Him to give you ears that hear the words He wants you to hear. To be unhurried in His presence and to recognise His voice amidst a noisy and distracting world.

DAY 31

Being Like-Minded

I sometimes watch those TV shows where a (usually young) couple are looking for a new house to rent/buy. They are shown three properties and at the end of the program, they must choose one.

A budget is discussed beforehand as well as some 'must haves' and a few 'would likes'. What is fascinating to me is the number of times we follow two people who don't seem to be on the same page about what they want, or even what their priorities are. One will say that he won't compromise on the type of kitchen he is after, the other will talk about how she cannot live without a big garden. The letter 'I' is used much more than the word 'we'. The attempt between two individuals, who, in theory, love each other and have chosen to be together, to make a joint decision sometimes feels more like a struggle to bring peace between warring tribes.

The joys of working with others can be just as challenging in the church. Given Paul's instructions to the Philippian church on this subject, there may well have been some concerns here.

Paul writes in Phil 2: 1 – 4, '…if you have any encouragement from being united with Christ, if any comfort from his love, if any common sharing in the Spirit, if any tenderness and compassion, then make my joy complete by being *like-minded*, having the same love, being one in spirit and of one mind. Do nothing out of selfish ambition or vain conceit. Rather, in humility value others above yourselves, not looking to your own interests but each of you to the interests of the others'.

What does it mean to be like-minded with others or with another?

I don't think it means to be a clone of someone else, or even that you agree on everything. Perspectives, experiences and interests will always vary between any two or more people. Paul knows this, which is why this passage of Scripture is so helpful. The Philippian church is probably a good example of a community of diverse believers, with a successful and prominent local businesswoman (Lydia) trying to get on with an ex-fortune-telling (and very loud) slave girl, and a jailer.

Imagine building a house that is to become a home. God is building a spiritual home in Philippi; Paul laid the foundations through the preaching of God's Word in Acts 16: 11 – 40, and he draws attention to those foundations here in his letter.

He reminds them (and us) that it is Christ who unites us, and we share the same Spirit. God's presence amongst us must affect how we live, increasing for example compassion for each other. If we have the same love for Christ, and therefore a unifying spirit between us, then let's seek the blessing of others above our own wants. We can express our perspectives, experiences and opinions but in the context of a spiritual home where Christ is the head; and where we are constantly looking to meet the hopes and needs of those around us.

I don't know about you, but if that's the type of church Paul was building in Philippi, that's the kind of spiritual home I want to live in today.

Suggested prayer: Lord, when it comes to working or fellowshipping with other believers, help me to play my part in pursuing like-mindedness, seeking oneness in spirit, seeking to bless others and working to fulfill the interests of my brothers and sisters in Christ before my own. Amen.

DAY 32

How Much More

In Luke 18: 1 – 8, Jesus tells the story of an unjust judge and a widow. The widow was in desperate need of assistance. 'Grant me justice against my adversary,' she cried, as she banged on his door again, and the next day, and the next.

Eventually the judge caved in and he granted her request, so this is a story about perseverance, right?

At the end of the story Jesus concluded with: However, when the Son of Man comes will He find faith on the earth (Luke 18: 8). So, is this a story about faith?

I think this is a parable about something even deeper.

Being a widow in first century Palestine, she had no rights. She may well have had no one to plead for her, no protector, and no other family member to care for her. With no money the widow would have been in no position to bribe the judge. She was pleading with a judge who didn't care. She was asking help from one who had no fear of God, and who would give no promises.

There is another parable a few chapters back from this (Luke 11: 5 – 8) which has some similarities to this one. Here, someone goes to a friend in the middle of the night, asking for bread to feed an unexpected guest. The friend is already tucked up in bed and doesn't want to get up. 'No' is not taken for an answer and there is some to-ing and fro-ing until the friend finally pulls himself out from under the covers and reluctantly passes on the bread. Another story about perseverance, right?

Maybe, except it is followed by v 9 – 12 about asking God for things and this: 'If you then, though you are evil, know how to give good gifts to your children, how much more will your Father in heaven give the Holy Spirit to those who ask him!' (Luke 11: 13)

How much more. Jesus is teaching us that our Father in heaven is a 'how much more' God.

What do we know about our Father in heaven? He's our Father, He loves us, He's for us not against us, and He has chosen us, He sent His son, Jesus, to die on that cross for us, He's got a purpose for each of our lives, and He's promised to provide our every need.

So, if we know how to look after those that we care for, how much more will He look after us; how much more will He hear our prayers, hear our pleas for justice, and hear our cries for help? I think Luke 18: 1 – 8 is a 'how much more' story.

Let's compare God the Father to the unjust judge. The judge had no fear of God (v 2) – our Father *is* God. The judge had no compulsion to do the right thing. No conscience. On the other hand, Ps 145: 17 tell us, 'The Lord is righteous in all his ways; and faithful (or kind) in all he does'.

The judge didn't give two hoots about people, or what they thought. On the other hand, Ps 86: 15 tells us that God is abounding in steadfast love and faithfulness towards his people. And the judge seemed unmotivated by injustice – he didn't care! Yet God, we are told, in Ps 33: 5 *loves* justice.

In other words, it is not about how much or little faith you have (Jesus said a mustard seed is enough) and it is not so much about being a person who perseveres, it is much more about *who* we are praying to – a 'how much more' God.

Don't look at the size of your faith; look at the character of your God!

Suggested prayer: Lord, thank you that you are a 'how much more' God. You are righteous and faithful in all you do; you love justice, and you abound in steadfast love. Thank you that I don't need to keep banging on the door of a god who doesn't hear or care. You are a God who loves to give good things and the Holy Spirit to those who ask him. Amen.

DAY 33

But I Grew up with this Guy

Jesus grew up in Nazareth and in the book of Mark chapter six we find Him visiting His hometown. Like any good Jew, he went to the synagogue on the Sabbath and he immediately assumed the role of Rabbi and started teaching, even though many in the same room would only have known Him as a simple tradesman.

No wonder they asked, 'Where did this man get these things? What is this wisdom that has been given him? What are these remarkable miracles he is performing? Isn't this the carpenter? Isn't this Mary's son and the brother of James, Joseph, Judas and Simon? Aren't his sisters here with us?' (Mark 6: 2-3)

We are then told these chilling words, 'and they took offense at him'.

In other words, Jesus is just a guy like us. Who does he think he is?

The town who had helped raise Jesus during the first 30 years of His life failed to recognise who He really was, and His words and actions were an affront to them.

Mark then tells us that Jesus was *amazed* at their lack of faith (Mark 6: 6). It takes a lot for the Son of God to be amazed at anything. How sad that it was precipitated by unbelief - by those who, perhaps, should have known Him.

On another occasion, Jesus was amazed by a person who *did* express faith - a Roman centurion. The commander of soldiers, whose servant had recently become paralyzed, simply declared to Jesus, 'all you need do, Jesus, is speak the word and my servant will be healed, just like ordering obedient soldiers into action' (Matt 8: 8 – 9, my paraphrase).

Obviously, the centurion hadn't grown up with Jesus! Because if he had, perhaps he might have grown so familiar with him as to become blind to who He was.

The trouble is, when someone has been in our life for a long time, we think we know them. More often than not, we have just become used to them being around. If that can happen with Jesus, how much more might we make inaccurate judgments about others - about that work colleague we have known since the beginning; about my brother, my sister, or that person I hung out with at school.

But God is in the business of surprises. I believe He loves to show us His creative power and, in particular, He loves to show us what He can do in and through a human being whose heart is after Him. Especially those we might have given up on. Even those who may have let us down. Especially those who have let us down. Let us not limit God by the poor imagination that comes with familiarity.

You might have known that person for a long time, but God may well have some new and wonderful plans for them. You may think you have an accurate picture of him/her, but only God knows their true potential.

Suggested prayer: Has this devotion made you think of someone you may have given up on? Someone you find hard to forgive; someone who continues to make poor choices. Try to see them as a child of God who has great potential in Him. Pray that they may begin to walk into the purposes God has for them.

DAY 34

God will do what He said He will do

Have you ever read the book of 1 Samuel? This is the book in the Bible that introduces us to the boy who would kill Goliath and become Israel's greatest king – David. It is a story of faith, failure, triumph and tragedy. King Saul is on a collision course with disaster and David must cling to God's promises if he is to experience them coming to pass.

For me, there is one message that rings out throughout the book loud and clear: God will do what He has said He will do.

God gave the people of Israel a king. God told him through the prophet Samuel that He will appoint him leader over Israel and, of course, He did, but after King Saul failed to obey God, he was informed that the royal line will no longer continue through his family. In fact, another king will be chosen. David was secretly appointed and anointed half-way through the book.

In contrast to Saul, David understood the certainty of God's promises and he sought to trust God and obey Him. Even at his lowest point in the Cave of Adullam when the armies of Israel were hunting him down, led by a jealous and angry Saul, David declared that God is the one who 'fulfills his purposes for me' (Ps 57: 2)

In other words, God will do what He has said He will do.

And that's a promise for us today. If you are a follower of Jesus like me, then you stand at the other side of the cross to David – forgiven through repentance and faith, and now with a whole new set of promises.

Jesus told us that he will never leave us, he will never drive us away because we belong to Him (John 6: 37). If we take prayer seriously, developing our relationship with the Father in the secret place, we will be rewarded (Matt 6: 6). If we seek first His Kingdom and His righteousness, then all our needs will be met (Matt 6: 33), and so much more.

I have a pin-board on the wall of my study and over the years I have attached verses that have spoken to me, helpful thoughts that have come through prayer and prophetic words spoken over me by others. I consider them promises from God and every now and then I will read them afresh and cling to them.

Why? Because, like David, I believe God is the one who fulfills His promises for me.

When the tough times come, when there are Goliaths still to kill and when there is nothing we can do but just sit in the secret place and wait, one thing is sure: God will do what He has said He will do.

Suggested prayer: Lord, thank you for the truth that you are a God who keeps His promises. You fulfill the words you have spoken. Lord, you know the things I find difficult and the challenges I face so I trust you to do the things you have said you will do. Amen.

DAY 35

Looking Forward to Heaven

I'm not big on the idea of dying.

I was thinking about that the other day. I even found myself trying to imagine what it might feel like to be close to death. It was not a happy thought. I shook my head, shivered slightly and tried to think of something else.

Then I started reading 1 Corinthians chapter 15 and something hit me.

The first half of the chapter is taken up with Paul's impassioned plea to the Corinthian church that they have no doubt in their minds of Jesus Christ's resurrection from the dead. 'If Christ has not been raised', he says, 'our preaching is useless and so it your faith' (1 Cor 15: 14). If Jesus did not rise from the dead, then our sins are not forgiven, and we will have no hope for the future.

However, continues Paul, Jesus *did* rise from death and so we, by faith in Him, will also pass from death to life. It is a glorious certainty.

We still have to die, though. That's the bit I don't like.

Next Paul starts talking about the resurrected body – what our existence will be like in the life to come. We will have a heavenly body, but according to Paul, this will be as different to our present body as the sun is to the moon (v 41).

Paul has received insight about some curious details: The resurrected body will be imperishable; it cannot decay or develop a terminal illness. There will be no more suffering (mentioned in Rev 21: 4) and we won't die.

The resurrected body will have power – I don't know that that means except Paul also describes it as a spiritual body (v 44), one that bears a likeness to Jesus himself. In the gospels and the early chapters of the book of Acts, we find Jesus' resurrected body appearing and disappearing and ascending into the sky. The mind boggles!

Putting all of this together, beyond death we will have a body that does not malfunction, that is immortal, imperishable, powerful and spiritual in nature, perhaps even with abilities we can only dream about here on Earth. You and I are going to have great bodies in Heaven!

And then it hit me. For the change to take place, from the natural to the spiritual, from the perishable and failing, to the imperishable and glorious, my earthly body has to die. As a seed effectively dies when it is buried in the ground to produce something new and beautiful, we too must die for the next life to begin.

Death is simply a door to a better life. A transition to something glorious. Like falling asleep and waking up in a new and better world.

Death may be painful and uncomfortable for some, but in Christ it is only the beginning of a better future.

Suggested prayer: Lord, thank you that you are a God of Hope. Life doesn't end in death but continues through a door to your presence. Thank you that although my earthly body will have reached its usefulness, you will give me a new body that is spiritual, imperishable, immortal and powerful. I look forward to eternal life with you. Amen.

DAY 36

Gathering and Reaping

In Exodus chapter 16, we come across the famous story about Manna.

The grumbling Israelite community accused Moses of starving them to death, and the Lord responded by promising to 'rain down bread from heaven for you' (Ex 16: 4).

Meat in the form of Quail was provided as the evening meal and then 'thin flakes like frost on the ground' (v 14) appeared every morning after the early dew had evaporated. Somebody said, 'Manna!', meaning 'what is it?' and the name stuck. Verse 31 tells us it was 'white like coriander seed and tasted like wafers made of honey'.

The Lord told His people to gather only what they needed for each day. No hoarding! Plus, twice the amount the day before the Sabbath. No collecting was allowed on the Sabbath. Eating manna every morning was strongly connected to obedience. Even in the area of eating they were to do only what God told them to do.

Many centuries later, Jesus sat by a well in Sychar in Samaria after talking to a woman about eternal life, and His disciples returned from a trip into town to buy food. They offered some to Him, but He refused saying, 'My food is to do the will of him who sent me and to finish his work' (John 4: 34). Again, food is connected here to obedience.

Needless to say, some of the Israelites did not do a good job of listening to God's instructions. Some collected more than they needed and kept the reminder overnight, but in the morning, it stank and was full of maggots. Some tried to find the flakes first thing on the Sabbath but there was none to be found. Doing things their own way meant wasted effort, a maggot infestation, and a bad smell!

On the other hand, when Jesus obeyed His Father, not only did the woman at the well find new hope, but the whole community came to believe His words. Jesus was in the right place at the right time, He did the will of His father and the sweet fragrance of Heaven filled the town.

It strikes me that, whatever type of ministry we might be involved with, we must want to do the will of the Father – whatever that is. It might mean not gathering too much (not over-extending ourselves), when He has said, 'this is sufficient for now'. It might mean not hanging on to something for longer than it was intended when maybe it's time to pass that ministry on.

When we gather according to His instructions, blessings don't become a bad smell. When we seek His will and are careful to do that faithfully, I believe the Lord will give us the fruit we hope for. It will be free, a sweet fragrance and satisfying.

esus said, 'Open your eyes and look at the fields! They are ripe for harvest... I sent you to reap what you have not worked for.' (John 4: 35, 38). Let's gather and reap according to His instructions and see the miracles He has got in store.

Suggested prayer: Take some time today to stop and pray. Ask the Lord to help you discern His will. Think about areas of your life, the responsibilities you carry, people you connect with and influence. Ask Him to show you the things He has called you to do, but also the things he has not called you to do.

DAY 37

Truth

My wife persuaded me to buy some new underwear recently.

When I got home, I opened the pack of seven briefs and noticed that each had, emblazoned around the elastic rim, large letters embroidered in to spell a day of the week.

Yesterday, being Tuesday, I wore the appropriate pair. Later in the afternoon I was talking on the phone with a friend who had just finished a stint of night shifts. He was trying to work out which day it was. I told him, but he was convinced it was Wednesday. In hindsight, I think I should have said, 'Look, I know it's Tuesday because I've just checked my underpants. My briefs are an authority in this matter, so just believe them.'

And that got me thinking about the notion of truth, and on what authority we base the things we believe. For example, I base my Christian worldview on the words of the Bible, but how do we know the Bible's got it right?

One argument is that we can *experience* the Bible to be true. We can find the wisdom the book encourages us to pray for; we can read the stories and stumble across a detail that speaks to us personally; we can meditate on the descriptions of God and discover the peace we have been searching for. However, those outside the faith may well claim that they have found inspiration though sources other than the Bible.

So, another argument is historical authenticity of Jesus. Outside of the Bible there are accounts of a man who did, 'surprising deeds' (*Jewish Antiquities*, Josephus) and many old portions of the Bible in their original Greek text still exist today.

I think what nails it for me, though, is the extraordinary transformation of eleven men. Jesus' twelve disciples (minus one) were in fear for their lives. Their mentor and rabbi had been brutally put to death by Roman soldiers and, as far as they knew, the powers-that-be were after them too. Locked in a room, afraid and out of sight, John's gospel tells us that they suddenly saw Jesus and spoke with Him. That was just the beginning.

Six weeks later they had an encounter with the Holy Spirit and, following that, they spent the rest of their lives telling the world that Jesus had returned to life. Most of them eventually and willingly died as a direct result of that belief.

What can cause such a turn-around and create such courage in once-fearful hearts? To me, the resurrection of Christ and the power of the Holy Spirit are the only things that make sense.

Large chunks of the Bible were written by those caught up in the middle of all this and they, along with Jesus Himself, were happy to endorse the rest as 'God-breathed' (2 Tim 3: 16) – inspired by God.

So, on what do you base your beliefs? Be careful! If there is no solid foundation, they may be as flimsy as a pair of underpants!

Suggested prayer: Set aside some today to thank God for His Word – the Bible. Thank Him for the stories, the wisdom contained within its pages and the verses that particularly speak to you. Ask for His help in continuing to read and study its contents regularly and for the rest of your life.

DAY 38

Looking for Peace

I can't seem to find any peace at the moment.

'Turn from evil and do good' (Ps 34: 12)

What do you mean turn from evil and do good? Can you be more specific?

'Make sure that nobody pays back wrong for wrong, but always strive to do what is good for each other and for everyone else' (1 Thess 5: 15)

What does this have to do with peace?

'Turn from evil and do good
seek peace and pursue it' (Ps 34: 12)

'Consider the blameless, observe the upright;
a future awaits those who seek peace' (Ps 37: 37)

So, to find peace, first I have to seek it in my relationships with others?

'Make every effort to do what leads to peace and to mutual edification' (Rom 14: 19)

'If it is possible, as far as it depends on you, live at peace with everyone' (Rom 12: 18)

Live at peace with everyone? I'm not sure I can do that. You don't know what I have to live with. She is always so picky; he's got a mouth the size of a crater and everyone knows the guy over there is hard work.

'Blessed are the peacemakers, for they will be called children of God' (Matt 5: 9)

'Peacemakers who sow in peace, reap a harvest of righteousness' (James 3: 18)

OK, I'll give it a try, although I have never seen myself as a peacemaker. Will God help me?

'The Lord gives strength to his people;
the Lord blesses his people with peace' (Ps 29: 11)

'I can do all things through him who strengthens me' (Phil 4: 13)

But what about my own peace? There is a lot of turmoil in my heart. Sometimes I feel so worried and stressed. What do I do about that? Shouldn't I sort myself out first?

'Peace I leave with you; my peace I give you. I do not give to you as the world gives. Do not let your hearts be troubled and do not be afraid' (John 14: 27)

OK, Lord, you promise to give me peace. Please give me the peace I need, please help me to trust you with the things that make me anxious.'

'Do not be anxious about anything, but in every situation, by prayer and petition, with thanksgiving, present your requests to God. And the peace of God, which transcends all understanding, will guard your hearts and your minds in Christ Jesus' (Phil 4: 6 – 7)

Suggested prayer: Lord, help me to be a peace-maker. To work always towards what is good and seek peace with those around me. And Lord, help me, daily, to lift my troubles to you in prayer and trust that I may experience your peace in my heart and mind. Amen.

DAY 39

A Spacious Place

In Psalm 18, David expresses, with enormous gratitude, praise to God who has granted him a significant victory over his enemies.

Things were not looking good for him – 'the cords of death entangled me; the torrents of destruction overwhelmed me' (Ps 18: 4). An early death was frighteningly close and so David called out to the Lord in desperation (v 6).

The future king's deliverance was swift and decisive, and David was subsequently unrestrained in his praise to the Lord, describing God's intervention with a variety of vivid metaphors - the Lord thundered out of the brightness of his presence with hailstones and lightening (v 12 – 13); mountains shook (v 7), and fire blazed as the heavens parted (v 8 – 9).

We imagine David cornered in the battle by strong enemy soldiers until the Lord, 'reached down from on high' and granted him an unlikely victory. No longer trapped, David was brought out 'into a spacious place' (19) – a place of freedom and victory.

Tremper Longman III in his commentary on the Psalms helpfully suggests that Christian readers can apply these words to their situation today as we engage, daily, in spiritual battle against, 'the powers of this dark world' (Eph 6: 12).

So how might we interpret a 'spacious place' for us in the 21st century?

We, too, were once cornered in battle, not just entangled by the threat of death, but *actually dead* in our transgressions and sins as Paul makes in clear in Eph 2: 1. God reached down from on high, and through Christ's death on the cross, 'made us alive' again (Eph 2: 5). A simple expression of repentance and faith on our part was all that was needed for God to pour out an abundance of mercy, forgiveness and grace.

So, where is the spacious place?

Paul continues in Ephesians 2: 6, 'God raised us up with Christ and seated us with him in the heavenly realms in Christ Jesus'. No longer trapped and heading towards eternal death, our new place is next to the Father. So, just as David was able to turn the battle around from the vantage of his new spacious place (Ps 18: 37 – 42), we now fight from our new position, 'in Christ'.

Here we are very close to the Father, every prayer is before Him, His presence fills the air and there is victory over sin and death (1 Cor 15: 56 – 57). We are free to get up from the battle floor and with new energy pick up the sword and use it again with His strength, just as David did in Ps 18: 39, 'You armed me with strength for battle; you made my adversaries bow at my feet'.

A spacious place is not necessarily a one free from conflict, but it is a place where we dwell in the throne room of God, where we can, 'be strong in the Lord and in his mighty power' (Eph 6: 10).

Suggested prayer: If you are a follower of Jesus, forgiven and set free through faith in Christ's death on the cross, think about your new spacious place. You are 'in Christ', close to the Father and dwelling in the throne room of God. With these truths in view, bring your praise and requests to God.

DAY 40

Bread and Wine

When we read the stories of the Last Supper in the Gospels, it is worth noting that the disciples had no idea what was going on!

2,000 years later, we can talk about Judas, the man who was about to betray Jesus and give the authorities an easy chance to arrest Him for a small bribe. Today, we know that it was all part of God's plan and Jesus knew that too.

2,000 years later we can imagine Jesus breaking the loaf and we can reflect on that act as a symbol of His body being broken, and life being taken from Him as he was nailed to the cross. We can see Him pouring wine into a cup as a metaphor of His blood being shed for the forgiveness of our sins, just like a bull, a goat or a lamb in the temple.

We can even mark that particular Passover celebration as a moment in time when new meaning emerged from the Exodus story like a butterfly from a chrysalis because Jesus' death on the cross will become a new day of God's deliverance from sin and evil.

But the disciples did not understand a bar of it!

Jesus had tried to tell them, of course, on a number of occasions, that He was headed to Jerusalem, where He would be killed, and on the third day rise from the dead.

On one notable occasion, Peter simply couldn't handle it, saying, 'Never Lord! This shall never happen to you!' Prompting Jesus' shocking and now famous response: 'Get behind me, Satan... you do not have in mind the concerns of God, but merely human concerns' (Matt 16: 23).

Peter and the 12 didn't get it then, so it is unlikely anything had changed by the time they reached the Passover meal. The disciples still had no clue as to what was about to happen to Jesus, they didn't realise that this is the last time they will eat together, and so they also didn't know what this Last Supper represented.

But these men trusted their Rabbi and Master and so they went along with it. They did what He asked them to do – they ate the bread and drank the wine, believing it was just another regular festival, same as last year.

It was only after Jesus rose from the dead that things started to make sense.

It strikes me that there are times when we don't understand everything either. There are seasons when we have questions, uncertainties, and, sometimes, unexplained heartaches in our lives. We come to church, we gather with friends and we share and take communion.

Why do we do that? Perhaps because it is something we do regularly, it is part of church life, perhaps it is because our Lord and Master, Jesus, has told us to. But maybe it is also our way of saying we trust Him, and we believe that one day the questions, uncertainties and heartaches will make more sense.

So, let me suggest, next time you receive the bread and wine to remember Christ's death on the cross, consider doing the following: Acknowledge that you may not know all the answers, but thank Him for dying on the cross anyway. Tell Him where you are struggling, but then as you eat the bread and drink the wine say, 'Lord I trust you. I don't know how things are going to work out, but I trust you'.

Suggested prayer: Lord, I don't understand everything, but you have all knowledge and wisdom. Lord, you know all the things I am struggling with, but I put my trust in your love, your power and your sovereignty over all things. Amen.

DAY 41

God can use Anyone

Everyone thought they would fail.

Within weeks of Paul and his team arriving in Thessalonica with the good news of Jesus, those who had come to faith were left without leaders, facing persecution and under intense pressure to recant their faith.

Paul, Silas and Timothy had been forced to leave. Those opposed to this new Christian faith had persuaded some local troublemakers to stir up the assembled crowd with lies about the team. They had no choice but to go.

Paul was desperate to return. "When we were torn away from you for a short time… out of our intense longing we made every effort to see you" (1 Thess 2: 17). However, for reasons unclear, they weren't able to get back until Timothy finally made the journey on his own.

In an age with no mobile phones or internet connection, the wait for news must have been excruciating. Had the church survived the persecution? Were they still meeting? With the longest standing church members barely a few weeks old in the faith on the day Paul and the team left, did they have any leaders? Who was taking care of these baby Christians?

Eventually Timothy returned with the welcome news that the church had indeed survived and their faith was still strong. The young Christians were standing firm despite the challenges around them, but that wasn't all. To Paul's joy and amazement, not only were the Thessalonian believers still meeting as a church, but they were reaching out to their local community with the message of the risen Christ, to the wider area and even beyond. In fact, their passion for evangelism was the talk of the town for miles around (1 Thess 1: 7 – 8).

What was their secret?

In the same first letter to the Thessalonians, we get some insights: The baby Christians knew they were hand-picked by God; the gospel had made a deep impact in their lives and they had experienced God's supernatural power (1 Thess 1: 4 – 5). None of them had been mentored with leadership training, none of them could boast any kind of spiritual heritage, but despite their lack of knowledge and skill, God used them.

If we were to look for examples of spiritual maturity in the pages of the New Testament, we might point to well-known characters like Paul, or Peter, or those trained under them; those who have been faithful in serving God over many years, in which case you can forget the Thessalonians. They don't qualify.

And yet Paul tells us they had become a model church to all others within hundreds of miles.

Now, I don't want to minimise the importance of education, training and the maturity that comes with years of serving God, but maybe God can use anybody for His purposes, especially those who have experienced God's love and power and the deep impact of the Gospel. I, for one would like some of the joy and zeal of these baby Christians to rub off on me.

Suggested prayer: Think about the Thessalonians' experience of God. They knew that they were chosen; the gospel made a deep impact in their hearts and lives and they experienced God's supernatural power. Draw near to God and pray the same things for yourself and for those in your care.

DAY 42

He Watches over You

You know that annoying moment? You are finally talking to that person you've been wanting to meet for some time. The conversation is going well, but wait, they seem distracted by something else in the room, they are not actually listening to you.

How rude!

But then, later, you realise you've done that to people as well.

How embarrassing!

Psalm 121: 4 tells us that the Lord neither slumbers nor sleeps. The implication is that He never even loses focus, not for a moment. A guard on night shift may slumber at his post, drifting into a light sleep or lose concentration, but not the Lord.

Here in Western Australia, we often see signs on the sides of long country roads which read, 'Driving tired can kill'. A brief closing of the eyes or even just a momentary lapse of attentiveness can end very badly. I remember a relative of mine telling me once that she was driving her car with a heaviness in her eyes along a long, empty stretch of road in the UK. Suddenly, she woke up, shocked that she had fallen asleep at the wheel just in time to slam on her brakes in front of a truck.

Verses three and five of Psalm 121 tell us that God, who is always fully alert, watches over us. As we lift up our eyes to Him (v 1) and put our trust in Him for all we need, the promises are outstanding: He 'will not let our foot slip' (v 3), He will protect us, and He will keep us from harm. He will watch over our lives, all our comings and goings, today and every day (v 7 – 8).

And, by the way, He's not taking any time off. Mary Crowley, a Christian and one of the leading businesswomen in the US in the 1970s said: 'Every evening I turn my worries over to God. He's going to be up all night anyway.'

God never sleeps, He doesn't need to, and if He never takes a nap or falls into a daydream, He is more than capable of watching over our every circumstance. 'The sun will not harm you by day' (v 6) – the harmful affects of the sun in the heat of the day or, indeed, any perils that may befall the pilgrim will not touch you; 'nor the moon by night' (same verse) – the fears that may come in the dark or at night have no claim on you.

The One who cannot die, take a siesta or float off into a dream world gives you His full attention and watches over your life.

That means you can trust Him with it.

Suggested prayer: Lord, thank you for always being awake and alert. You never drift off to sleep or lose concentration. Therefore, I can trust you with my life. You see everything that goes on and you watch over every circumstance. You are more than capable of protecting me from the dangers and fears that come my way. Amen.

DAY 43

Is the Lord's Arm too Short?

I don't like the sound of people crying.

When I see someone in distress, I just want to go over and put an arm around them and say, 'There, there! It's going to be ok, shhhh! Please stop – you're upsetting me!' So, I wonder how Moses felt during the following incident.

About a year after leaving Egypt, and shortly after their stay at Mount Sinai, the people of God started complaining to Moses about the restaurant choice. Only 'manna' was on the menu, described as something that tasted like coriander seed.

"If only we had meat to eat! We remember the fish we ate in Egypt at no cost—also the cucumbers, melons, leeks, onions and garlic. But now we have lost our appetite; we never see anything but this manna!" (Num 11: 4 – 6)

The situation was so bad that the author of Numbers describes whole families, sitting at the entrances to their tents *wailing*. Yes, wailing. Not just shedding a few tears, but actually wailing!

The text tells us that the Lord was very angry, and Moses was troubled. I bet he was! Moses had no idea what to do and so the Lord took over. God first told Moses to gather 70 of Israel's elders to share the burden of leadership, and then to address the whole community, telling them that meat is on its way.

What happens next is interesting. A private conversation between the Lord and Moses takes place but then ends with Moses spluttering, 'What! How on earth are you going to do that?' (My paraphrase) Or 'How on earth are you going to find enough meat to feed all these people?' To which, God gives the well-known response, 'Is the Lord's arm too short?' (Num 11: 23)

What a strange phrase!

In a nutshell, God's arm was a common metaphor in the Scriptures to describe His power to intervene in the affairs of human beings (e.g., Ps 98: 1 – 2). Earlier, before the exodus from Egypt, God had promised He would redeem His people with an 'outstretched arm' (Ex 6: 6). Later Moses marvels at the works of God in Deut 4: 34, boasting miracles, signs and wonders, 'by a mighty hand an outstretched arm.'

A long, outstretched arm is one which can do anything. Moses was already familiar with the phrase, so to ask the question, 'Is the Lord's arm too short?' was gentle chastisement from the Lord, in effect saying 'Come on Moses, you have seen my glory and my power – I have a very, very long arm! Has my arm suddenly shrunk? Why have you stopped believing in me?'

Perhaps there are times when we also need that gentle chastisement, that reminder of who is in charge and how powerful He is. Next time we are tempted to sink into doubt, ask yourself this question, 'Is the Lord's arm too short?'

Suggested prayer: Think about the challenges you face or difficult situations you or those in your care have to deal with. Then ask the question, "Is the Lord's arm too short?" Think about specific miracles that God has performed throughout the pages of Scripture and then pray words of praise to Him. Think again about the things you are asking God for. Thank Him for His glory, power and outstretched arm.

DAY 44

He Delights in You

There are some words that always carry negative connotations for me.

For example, 'discipline' reminds me of a strict scout leader I knew many decades ago who seemed to have lost the word 'fun' from his dictionary. When I think of the word 'discipline' I think of standing to attention, saluting and shiny shoes.

The writer of the book of Hebrews doesn't shirk from the unpleasantness of discipline but he has an interesting spin on it.

For example, when we go through tough times, the Lord allows it, but He allows it because we are His children: 'Endure hardship as discipline; God is treating you as sons' (Heb 12: 7). Why would He do that?

Verses 10 and 11 go on to describe some of the good that might result from such times – peace, a harvest of righteousness and a sharing in God's holiness.

Certainly, many of us can testify to circumstances that God used to change something in us. I know for me, that when I am facing something hard, my inability to control the situation can be enough to drive me to the place of prayer and again ask for help. That challenges me to contemplate my frailty and His sovereignty. I know I am different today because of times God has formed something good in me though a season of prayer during a difficult season.

That's not all though: Verse 11 speaks of a harvest of righteousness. God is allowing hardship to occur in order to produce a harvest. What does that mean?

Some commentators suggest it refers to changes in our character. Certainly, the Scriptures promise us the miracle of transformation into the likeness of Christ as we meditate on God and His glory (2 Cor 3: 18). Others suggest an increase of self-control, or a new devotion to God.

It is probably different for each person and a mixture of all three but remember this: God does not discipline us because He is a harsh taskmaster. He disciplines us because we are His children and He sees what we might become.

There is one more thing. The writer of the book of Hebrews compares human fathers with God: human fathers will discipline their children for their good, so how much more will God? Human fathers love their children so how much more does God? In other words, 'The Lord disciplines those he *loves*' (Heb 12: 6).

The writer has borrowed the phrase from the book of Proverbs, quoting chapter 3: 11 – 12, but there is one word in Proverbs not present in the book of Hebrews, the word, 'delight'. 'The Lord disciplines those he loves, as a father the son he delights in'. 'Delight' adds yet another layer to the picture God is painting here.

When we go through tough times, God uses the painful season for our good. There is a harvest to come. As we meditate on Him, trust and obey His Word, we give Him permission to form our character to be more like His Son, Jesus.

It may be painful, but He does this because we are His children, those He loves – those He delights in.

Think about that: The Lord delights in us. While He is disciplining us, He is delighting in us.

God made us, and He loves to see us transformed into the image of His Son. Tough situations may come our way, but God uses them for our good, and He is personally present - delighting in each son and daughter every step of the way.

Suggested prayer: Lord, thank you that you use tough times to bring discipline – not to harm us or discourage us but to bring about a fruitful harvest in our hearts and lives. Thank you that I am a dearly loved child of God and you delight in me. Please use my tough times to transform me to be more like Jesus. Amen.

DAY 45

God Knows You by Name

The book of Numbers in the Bible does not kick off like a best-seller. For several chapters, we have instructions for camping and marching, lists of tribes and clans, oh… and numbers – lots of numbers!

However, everything in these pages is inspired by God. The first three words of the book are, 'The Lord Spoke.' So, the content these early chapters must be important. What did the Lord say?

After Moses had received the 10 commandments plus the detailed plans for the building of the tabernacle, he and the Israelites were still camped at Mount Sinai, but ready to hear The Lord's next instructions.

It had been over a year since the nation escaped the clutches of Egypt, 'with signs and wonders, by a mighty hand and an outstretched arm and with great terror' (Jer 32: 21). God had worked an incredible deliverance and had brought them to this place where they would begin to be shaped into a nation of their own.

But they wouldn't stay at Mount Sinai. The Lord had given them the law and, through the tabernacle, a way to search their hearts and atone for sin, but they would need to travel some distance on foot to claim the land that He had promised them. So, before setting off, God had one more direction: 'Take a census' (Num 1: 2) – take a census of the whole Israelite community (that's a lot of people!), recording clans, families and individuals.

At surface level, the first chapter is just a list of names and numbers, but something struck me as I read the 50 or so verses that followed - God knew people by name.

In verse two, He told Moses to 'list every man by name, one by one'. Then, in verses four and five, God's instructions became very specific as He singled out tribal heads who will assist Moses in the task, individually recognising each one and the family they belong to. God didn't just know Moses by name,

He knew the entire Israelite community.

This reminds me of Jesus' comments in Matthew 10 (and Luke 12). In the middle of a confronting discourse about standing firm and speaking boldly in the midst of persecution, Jesus changed His tone to one of a gentle shepherd, addressing the natural fear that would arise in such a situation and telling them that sparrows, worth little in the marketplaces are never unnoticed by our Father in Heaven. How much more, then, are we?

In fact, said Jesus, 'Even the very hairs of your head are all numbered' (Matt 10: 30).

If He knows me by name, and he knows exactly how many hairs sit on my head, then He must know about my health issues and the worries that occupy my mind. He must see my needs and He is present when I don't know what to do and when I need His help.

If He knows me by name, then He knows how to take care of me.

> 'But now, O Jacob, listen to the Lord who created you.
> O Israel, the one who formed you says,
> "Do not be afraid, for I have ransomed you.
> I have called you by name; you are mine' (Is 43: 1 NLT).

Suggested prayer: Lord, thank you for knowing me by name. I am not just a number or a random person in your Kingdom, but I am known and loved by you. And if you notice even small details like the numbers of hair on a person's head, then you then you see all my needs and I can trust you to take care of them. Amen.

DAY 46

Content to be a Child

'So, what do you do?'

This is a standard question at parties - at least the ones I get invited to. I remember being asked this in a previous life when I was working as a high school teacher. 'I'm a teacher', I replied. 'Oh, you poor thing' was the immediate response. She wasn't finished.

'What subject do you teach?'

'Physics and general science.'

'Oh, how awful!'

There's not a lot you can say after that.

Where do you find your sense of worth? Some of us describe ourselves by what we do. I am a teacher, an engineer, a nurse etc. It doesn't matter that we are complex beings, with other interests, passions, experiences and so on. I am an engineer and that's what I am because that is what I do.

For some, what others think or say about us can somehow defines us. I have over 1400 friends on Facebook. My wife says I cannot possibly know that many people, let alone be friends with all of them. She is right, of course, and a good proportion of them have been people I have met just once or twice, or don't know that well. However, the sad part is that every time I post something, I want every one of those friends to 'like' it. I believe I am 'successful' if others notice me or approve of me. Tell me I'm not the only one!

And then there is what we have. We are what we drive or the clothes we wear or how big our office is. I know I'll really *be* something when I can afford that two-story house over by the lake.

Jesus did not allow Himself to be defined by what He did, what others said about Him or by what He had, but He did talk a lot about His Father in heaven.

When Jesus was baptized and the assembled crowd heard the audible voice of God, it is interesting to note what the Father *didn't* say. He didn't say, 'this is my son, he is the second person of the Trinity, he is the Word and he's had that role since the beginning'. He didn't say, 'this is my son, you should hear what the angels say about him'. He didn't say, 'this is my son, and as King of Kings and Lord of Lords, his wealth is impossible to imagine.' The Father simply said, 'You are my Son, whom I love; with you I am well pleased" (Mark 1: 11).

I think Jesus was content with that.

The Bible tells us that we are children of God, deeply loved by the Father.

Jesus encouraged His disciples – and therefore us - to do their 'acts of righteousness' in secret (Matt 6: 1 – 4) so that only the Father sees them. He instructed them (and us) to pray behind closed doors (Matt 6: 5 – 7) so that we pray to Him, and only Him. An audience of just one, the One that counts.

Are you a child of the Father? That's really all the self-worth you need.

Suggested prayer: Lord, thank you that you created me, and your love and power sustains me. Help me not to look in the wrong places for self-worth. Your Word tells me that I am your child, that you bled and died on the cross for me, and that you will never leave me. I have value because *you* value me. Amen.

DAY 47

Being Fat for Jesus

I once heard a friend of mine preaching a sermon where he encouraged us to all be FAT. Intrigued? He talked about being Faithful, Available and Teachable for Jesus. In a nutshell, he spoke about the importance of being Faithful to God's Word, Available to the promptings of the Holy Spirit and having Teachable hearts if we are going to fulfill the Great Commission.

Instead of the Great Commission, sadly, for many of us the call to 'go and make disciples in all nations' has become the Great Omission. We need to get the kids ready for school, that report should have been done yesterday, there are jobs promised and lists expanding. There isn't time. Business. Pressures. And then there's fear. We are afraid of getting it wrong, afraid of being labeled a religious nut, afraid of losing our friends. And so on.

What can we do about it?

Well, according to my friend, first, we can be Faithful: faithful to God's Word and faithful to His call upon our lives.

For example, God's Word encourages us to pray, right? How about trying this: Jesus instructed His disciples to pray for 'workers' to go into the harvest field (Matt 9: 38). So, when you have a spare moment, make a list of people you see regularly, who don't yet know Jesus. It can be a small list or a big list. Doesn't matter.

Then pray for them to have a heart open to God's influence and, here's the important bit: pray Matthew 9 verse 38, that God will send believers in Jesus ('workers') to 'cross their paths' – to meet them and influence them for Him. Tell me that's easy!

Second, my friend talked about being Available: Do you know Isaiah's powerful prayer in Isaiah 6: 8? 'Here I am, Lord; send me.' The Lord had called out to the heavenly host in His throne room, asking who would be willing to be God's hands and feet in a broken world. Isaiah responded in a heartbeat. He made himself available.

Maybe in our busyness we can pray for God's help in getting all the essential things done, but then pray that God will also use us to do His will to reach others for Christ? Oh, and add to that: pray that we will recognise the opportunities when they come.

Last, we can be Teachable: Don't listen to the voices that say, 'I'm not an evangelist' or 'this is not my skill set'. Listen to what God says, "I am the Lord, the God of all mankind. Is anything too hard for me?" (Jer 32: 27). It's not about what we can or can't do, it's much more about what *He can do through us*. I really like that verse because it means that God can use me. Even me!

And with those principles in our hearts, let's see what God can do. It's time to get F.A.T. Time to be F.A.T for Jesus.

Suggested prayer: Lord, I want to be faithful, available and teachable. I want to be faithful to your call upon my life and faithful to the things you teach me in Scripture. I also want to be available for you to use. Here I am, send me, please Lord. And Lord, grant me a teachable spirit. Help me focus not on what I can't do, but on what you can do through me. Amen.

DAY 48

Close to the Shepherd's Heart

Do you have go-to Bible Verses? You know what I mean – verses or passages or stories that you often find yourself reading if you are looking for comfort or encouragement.

I gravitate towards Isaiah 40 at such times.

There is something grand and majestic, yet deeply personal in this chapter. There are the early declarations of the coming of the Lord, when His glory will be revealed, and all will see it (v 5). Then in the middle of the chapter we face the greatness of who He is as we are reminded that the nations are like dust on scales in His hands (v 15) and how only He, the Lord, could stretch out the heavens as easily as drawing a pair of curtains (v 22).

He has all knowledge and all understanding; His Word stands forever, and He sits enthroned above His creation. The chapter is like a giant tapestry of God's magnificence.

Yet, interwoven in this tapestry, like small threads embroidered with painstaking detail, we find breath-taking glimpses of the Lord's love and care – 'those who hope in the Lord will renew their strength' (v 31) or 'speak tenderly to Jerusalem and proclaim to her that her hard service has been completed' (v 2).

In one such section of the canvas, a messenger of good news is instructed to shout at the top of his voice and proclaim that the sovereign Lord is coming with authority and power (v 9 – 10) but look at how the Lord is described in verse 11. He is like a shepherd, and an interesting detail is woven into the narrative - His lambs are not herded in droves or assembled on carts to follow at a distance, they are gathered in the shepherd's arms.

In fact, He Himself picks them up and holds them next to His chest and close to His heart, and, for those who must stay close to their mothers, 'he gently leads those who have young.'

If this is not a prophetic image of Jesus, I don't know what is!

But let's stay with Isaiah for a moment. The sovereign Lord who rules the universe holds His own close enough to hear His heartbeat and feel His breath.

In Ancient times, the shepherd would carry the lamb struggling to walk and he would hold the one who needs special guarding or care. The lamb who is exhausted or weary will find his strength returning in the warm embrace of the shepherd's strong arms.

You want to be close to the Shepherd's heart? Maybe it's time to stop running around and let Him pick you up and hold you for a while. Maybe you are exhausted enough to stop trying to do things in your own strength.

Maybe it's time to feel His breath and hear His heartbeat.

Because that's His desire too.

Suggested prayer: Lord, thank you that you are my shepherd. You are strong, faithful and loving. The power of the universe is in your hands, yet you love to hold me close to your chest. Close to your heart. Lord, I don't want to run myself into exhaustion, please help me to stop long enough in your presence to hear your heartbeat and know your will. Amen.

DAY 49

Deep Calls to Deep

In a Psalm that begins with a vivid description of a soul desperate for God ('As the deer pants for streams of water, so my soul pants for you O God' – Ps 42: 1), the psalmist commands his inner being to stay focused on the Lord, and then he says this:

'Deep calls to deep in the roar of your waterfalls' (Ps 42: 7).

Some commentators have interpreted this as a description of deep and dangerous waters from one source calling on deep trouble from another to unite against the Psalmist in his peril.

This certainly seems to be supported by the second part of verse seven: 'all your waves and breakers have swept over me'. As Shakespeare wrote in *Hamlet*, "When sorrows come, they come not single spies, but in battalions."

The psalmist might have found himself near a rapid river or thundering waterfall and he may have felt that the violent crashing of water on the rocks from all sides somehow mirrored his situation and inner turmoil.

But there is another way to read this.

The Psalmist has turned from addressing his soul to praying to the Lord in verse five, 'I will remember you' and he continues with 'all *your* waves and breakers have swept over me'. He doesn't blame God for his troubles, but he does recognise God's sovereignty and presence, even in the waves and breakers dashing against him. God is not the author of evil, but at the end of the day, the tumultuous waters still belong to Him.

And he interprets it as a call to deeper communion. He doesn't understand why God is allowing the suffering in his life (see v 9), but he commands his soul to put its hope in God and he makes a conscious decision to worship Him (v 11).

I remember at time when a person was stirring a considerable amount of trouble in a church I was pastoring. I was at my wit's end. On one particular morning, I could think of nothing to do except worship God, so that was what I did. The problem wasn't solved straight away, but something happened in my heart that morning which created a different perspective to the issue. I stopped trying to solve things myself and I put my hope in God.

The deeper the pain or the challenge, perhaps the deeper He draws us into relationship with Him – if we are willing. Deep *calls*… The Sovereign Lord over the trouble gently calls us. Perhaps His whispers can be heard above the cacophony of the crashing waters around us and despite the uncertainty of the situation we find ourselves in.

"Deep waters call out to what is deeper still; at the roar of your waterfalls" (ISV)

Suggested prayer: Lord, I want to go deeper with you. When the pain or challenges come, I don't want to quit or back away. Rather my heart wants deeper fellowship with you. Help me, in those times, to remember your sovereignty over all things and to catch your whispers of love over the cacophony of the battle. Amen.

DAY 50

Barriers to Faith

Have you ever wished you could get more faith? Buy a trolley load at the supermarket or dig up a lump of it from under the ground? And yet Jesus said, 'if you have faith as small as a mustard seed, you can say to this mountain, "Move from here to there", and it will move. Nothing will be impossible for you' (Matt 17: 20). For Jesus, just a tiny amount of faith in Him is all we need. So, what do we do when we don't feel have enough?

In Mark chapter nine, there is a story of a father of a demon-possessed boy, who came to Jesus and said, 'If you can do anything, take pity on us and help us.' Jesus took issue with the father's first three words. 'If you can?' He replied, 'Everything is possible for those who believe'. And then the father gave that famous response, 'I do believe; help me overcome my unbelief' (Mark 9: 24).

Without realising it, the father had identified something very important: 'I do believe (I have mustard seed faith), but please help me overcome my unbelief (help me overcome the thing that is getting in the way of my faith).

Here's something that might surprise you – you probably don't need more faith! But there are times when we might need to overcome things that are getting in the way - *barriers* to faith. The good news is Jesus can help us with that.

Just like he did with Jairus.

Jairus was a synagogue ruler who came to Jesus (in Mark 5: 22) and pleaded with Him to heal his very sick daughter. Jesus indicated to him that He would go to his house and minister to her, but they were interrupted. By the time they had got to the house, the girl was dead.

It would have been very easy for Jairus to give up at this point: the facts were clear – it was too late, and the girl had died. But Jesus said, 'don't be afraid;

just believe' (Mark 5: 36).

In just that moment Jesus confronted two major barriers to faith: facts and fear; or rather, doubts because of facts, and fear. Jesus wasn't asking Jairus to ignore the facts, and He wasn't asking him to psych up more faith. He was simply saying, 'look at me – look beyond the facts and the fear and believe in me.'

What are you praying for? Do the facts of the situation tell you it is impossible? Does fear try to take your attention away from God? If so, like looking through a dirty glass window to a glorious sunset, look beyond both of those things to Jesus. Look through them to the calm presence of the one who has authority over all things and who has all power. Then watch what God can do with that tiny mustard seed of faith.

Suggested prayer: What are you praying for? Do the facts of the situation tell you it is impossible? Does fear try to take your attention away from God? If so, like looking through a dirty glass window to a glorious sunset, look beyond both of those things to Jesus. Look through them to the calm presence of the one who has authority over all things and who has all power. Then pray. And watch what God can do with that tiny mustard seed of faith.

DAY 51

Be Strong and Take Heart

David trusts in his God. He describes Him as his rock and fortress (Ps 31: 3). "You are my God," he declares aloud (v 14), reminding himself of the Lord's unfailing love and goodness in the verses that follow.

At the beginning of Ps 31, David's prayers are those of a man in trouble. He asks God to deliver him, to hear his calls for help, come quickly to his rescue, be that rock of refuge and set him free from a situation in which he has become entrapped (v 1 – 5). He is in dire need.

The tough soldier and army commander has no qualms about wearing his emotions on the outside of his armour. He is in anguish (v 7, 10), distress (v 9), full of sorrow (v 9) and with his strength failing by the day. He describes his life as like broken pottery at the mercy of those who plot to take his life.

Next time I have a rough day, I might compare it to David's. It might not seem so bad.

I was struck by David's opening statement in this psalm, 'In you, O Lord, I have taken refuge'. The God of Israel is David's Lord who has proved His faithfulness and power on many occasions. David knows this, yet he still makes a choice to trust Him. God is a refuge, but David has *taken* refuge. David has made a conscious decision to step behind the Lord's protective shield – 'into your hands I commit my spirit' (v 5).

Jesus, of course, uttered these words, calling them out loudly to the Father seconds before he died on the cross (Luke 23: 46), an incredible moment of faith that the Father would not 'abandon him to the grave' (Acts 2: 27, 31 – 32 quoting Psalm 16), but that He would raise Him to life. In the weakness of the cross, we see the enormous strength of Christ's complete dependence on His Father in Heaven.

'In quietness and trust is your strength' (Is 30: 15)

Putting our hope in the Lord is not a sign of weakness, but a sign of fortitude. When all else fails and when the fragility of life (and the fragility of those around us) is most apparent, our hearts can find courage again in the promises of God – that He will deliver and provide safe shelter. We can look beyond the crumbling walls in view and remember the enduring pillars of His faithfulness over the years and throughout the ages.

No wonder David can end his lament with a cry to fellow believers, "Be strong and take heart, all you who hope in the Lord' (Ps 31: 24).

Suggested prayer: Lord, I choose to take refuge in you. You are faithful and all power is in your hands. Into those loving hands, I gladly place my life and I trust you for the future. Lord, you are my deliverer and my shelter, and I put my hope in you. Amen.

DAY 52

All That for Just One Person

Edward Kimball was a little-known Sunday school teacher in Detroit in the mid-nineteenth century. You have probably never heard of him.

On the other hand, you may have heard of the man in Mark chapter five – the scary one who was delivered from an army of demons. This miracle occurred straight after the dramatic calming of the storm at the end of chapter four, where the storm was so fierce that the disciples feared for their lives. Jesus simply told the storm to 'be still'. Later, on the other side of the lake, the first person Jesus met was the man with the evil spirits – Legion (5: 2). Then, after the man's deliverance, Jesus just got back in the boat again (5: 21) and left.

He did all of that for one man! The disciples must have been thinking, 'We went through all of that for just one crazy guy?'

Admittedly, Jesus might have stayed longer if the local inhabitants hadn't asked Him to leave, and maybe He might have ministered to many more, but it turns out that all of this really was for just one guy – and a massive rejection from the town council!

Have you ever felt you put lots of effort into what seemed like a tiny result? Perhaps you felt it was God's will to do that thing and you had high expectations, but the fruit seemed so minimal and the journey to get there so difficult.

If that describes you, I want to show you what happened to the man who was delivered - Legion. It's in verse 20 of chapter 5: It says he went back to the town to share his story and 'all the people were amazed'. This time they are not rejecting what Jesus has done, they are amazed what Legion says about Him. This is progress.

Actually, in Luke's telling of the story (Ch 8), we are told that the man went *all over town* to share how much Jesus had done for him and Mark tells us he went to the Decapolis. The Decapolis was 10 cities! He told his story in 10 cities. Jesus ministered to just one man and he in turn ministered to 10 cities.

Edward Kimball was a little-known Sunday school teacher in Detroit in the mid-nineteenth century. One day he visited an ordinary lad in his class, shared the Gospel of Jesus Christ with him and the lad gave his life to Christ. That young lad was D. L. Moody who would go on to lead millions of people to Christ, as well as found the Moody Bible Institute and The Moody Church in Chicago.

Edward Kimball went out of his way for one soul. Look where it led.

Let's never underestimate God's ability to multiply something we might do for just one person: a word of encouragement here; a gift there; a call to someone who is lonely; the sharing of your testimony to the guy on the bus; that small kindness that seems unnoticed by everyone else. In time, your single blessing to one may well become a multitude of blessings to many.

Suggested prayer: Who does God want you to bless today? Ask God to show you one thing that you might give to someone, however small. Then pray that God will multiply that gift through that person to others and to His glory.

DAY 53

Go Back to the Mountain

Someone once told me that if you are struggling to hear God's voice, or if you don't feel you can sense His leading, then go back to the last thing He spoke to you.

Elijah experienced the power of God in ways most of us can only imagine. On one occasion, the king (Ahab), accused him of being 'the troubler of Israel' (1 Kings 18: 17). Elijah, not one to back down even before the highest monarch in the land, then poured out a catalogue of wrongs committed by Ahab, including abandoning the Lord's commands and leading the nation into idol worship.

Elijah then challenged the king to a showdown. 'Bring me your best prophets of Baal and the nation will see who the real God is' (my paraphrase).

So, crowds of people showed up from all over the country along with 450 representatives of the idol, Baal. You know the story: the Baal prophets and Elijah each set up an altar with a dead bull on top and both sides called upon their god to ignite the sacrifice by fire from Heaven.

So confident was Elijah in the Lord's power, and the foolishness of idol worship, that He even started teasing the prophets as they grew more desperate for their god to hear them: 'Shout louder people, he's a god, isn't he? Maybe he's just busy today, perhaps he has dozed off, or is travelling somewhere' (1 Kings 18: 27, my paraphrase).

Elijah made his sacrifice even harder to ignite, with copious amounts of water, but after a short prayer, the fire of God exploded onto the scene, as the people fell on their faces exclaiming, 'The Lord – he is God!'

Elijah promptly had the prophets executed, prophesied an end to the nation's famine and ran like a wild sprinter to Ahab's hometown (Jezreel) just ahead of a heavy downpour.

Not bad for a day's work, except that in Jezreel, Elijah received word from the king's wife (Jezebel) that she will stop at nothing to ensure he is brutally executed.

Perhaps surprisingly, despite the miracles Elijah had just experienced, fear gripped his heart like a vice, and he ran for his life.

At first, the text of 1 Kings keeps us in suspense as to where he headed. He left his servant in Beersheba, then continued alone into the desert, praying with a fearful and discouraged heart that God might take him. Eventually, he arrived at Horeb. Why there?

The author of 1 Kings tells us that this is the mountain of God; it is the same place as Mount Sinai, where Moses received the ten commandments. Elijah hasn't run *away*; he has run *to* the place where God speaks. The man of God fled to the one location he knows where God words can be heard, to the place he hoped that God will speak again – to him.

At Elijah's lowest point (and even those who know God's love and power experience those times), where a dark cloud threatened to envelop his soul, Elijah found his way to the place of God's Word.

The good news is that God did indeed communicate with Elijah, and so the Lord can whisper words to you and me too. Perhaps we just need to go back to the mountain – to His Word. And for some of us, that might be going back to the last thing He said.

Suggested prayer: Next time you feel like running away, run to the Lord. Run to His Word. Ask the Lord today to help you build a reservoir of Biblical truth in your mind and heart, so that when the pressures come you can draw upon the truth God has deposited in you.

DAY 54

Hold Your Ground

Only let us live up to what we have already attained (Phil 3: 16).

What has God done in your life so far? When I think back over my time as a Christian up to today, I know that there have been significant moments – usually times of challenge or difficulty – when God has taught me something.

I remember reading *Prison to Praise* by Merlin R Carothers back in the 1970s and realising that God had given us the gift of language and song to express our faith in His greatness and goodness in the midst of the storm. Many a time, I have found new faith and joy spring up in my heart during such circumstances.

Then there was the realisation that giving thanks to God regularly, daily, was a powerful antidote to discouragement and disappointment.

I will always be grateful for the love God gave me for His Word – the Bible, and, like taking medicine each morning or eating a regular meal, as a young Christian I knew I needed His thoughts and wisdom dripping into my soul every day like clockwork.

In the letter to the Philippian church, Paul has already expressed his desire to know Christ, His power, and His righteousness, and to keep pressing on towards that goal, before encouraging the church to 'live up to what we have already attained'. Paul, like the church he is serving, has already learned some important life lessons. He knows that he, and they, still have a lot more to learn, but, in times of stress and difficulty, they must hold on to the things God has already taught them.

In other words, don't slip back when the going gets tough; don't fall back into old habits that God rescued you from. Put the life lessons and revelations into practice; keep building them into your life regularly, daily.'

'You've had some victories along the way; now hold your ground.'

When discouragements come, it is all too easy to slip into the comfortable, to slide back into seeking pleasures that might make you feel better for a while. You deserve them, don't you? Paul talks about this a few verses later, describing those who's god is their stomach, who's minds are drawn to things of the earth (Phil 3: 19). But he reminds the Philippians that they are now citizens of Heaven, able to stand firm in the faith, able to stay focused on the things God has impressed upon their hearts, able to stand their ground.

What would you say are the main things God has taught you since becoming a Christian? What changes have you made to your life since then? What gains have you made against our enemy, the devil, who wants nothing more than to drive you back to your old life? How has your life become shaped as a result of Christ dwelling in your heart?

If you are able to answer those questions, permit me one more: What do you need to do to hold your ground?

Suggested prayer: Lord, I want to be strong in you. As a citizen of Heaven and a child of the King, I want to stand firm in my faith in you. Please help me. Help me to remember the lessons you have taught me and the revelations you have given me and to stay focused on the things you have called me to do. Amen.

DAY 55

Grace

The Bible often talks about grace. What is it?

'I always thank my God for you because of his grace given you in Christ Jesus.' (1 Cor 1: 4)

So, it's a gift. Something given through faith in Jesus, right?

'For the law was given through Moses; grace and truth came through Jesus Christ.' (John 1: 17)

Well, I am a follower of Jesus, so I must have received grace when I started following Him. But what is grace?

'I am the least of the apostles and do not even deserve to be called an apostle, because I persecuted the church of God. But by the grace of God, I am what I am.' (1 Cor 15: 9 – 10)

'…in Christ we, though many, form one body, and each member belongs to all the others. We have different gifts, according to the grace given to each of us.' (Rom 12: 5 – 6)

It seems that grace has something to do with forgiveness, and something to do with gifts (or help) from Heaven. Is that correct?

'Let us then approach God's throne of grace with confidence, so that we may receive mercy and find grace to help us in our time of need.' (Heb 4: 16)

Why has God given us this grace?

'I do not set aside the grace of God, for if righteousness could be gained through the law, Christ died for nothing!' (Gal 2: 21)

'He has saved us and called us to a holy life—not because of anything we have done but because of his own purpose and grace.' (2 Tim 1: 9)

I understand. Grace is given that I might live a holy and right life, a life according to

His purposes. What sort of gifts does His grace include?

'With great power the apostles continued to testify to the resurrection of the Lord Jesus. And God's grace was so powerfully at work in them all.' (Acts 4: 33)

'We have different gifts, according to the grace given to each of us. If your gift is prophesying, then prophesy in accordance with your faith; if it is serving, then serve; if it is teaching, then teach; if it is to encourage, then give encouragement; if it is giving, then give generously; if it is to lead, do it diligently; if it is to show mercy, do it cheerfully.' (Rom 12: 6 – 8)

How do I begin to use these gifts of grace?

'Let your conversation be always full of grace, seasoned with salt, so that you may know how to answer everyone.' (Col 4: 6)

'Each of you should use whatever gift you have received to serve others, as faithful stewards of God's grace in its various forms. If anyone speaks, they should do so as one who speaks the very words of God. If anyone serves, they should do so with the strength God provides, so that in all things God may be praised through Jesus Christ.' (1 Pet 4: 10 – 11)

Suggested prayer: Spend time thanking God for His grace. For the forgiveness of your sins and the new life He has given you. Thank him for the many gifts He has given you, especially abilities and talents that you can use to bless others. Pray that He might show you new ways to use your gifts for His purposes.

DAY 56

On Things Above

Since then, you have been raised with Christ, set your hearts on things above, where Christ is seated at the right hand of God. Set your minds on things above, not on earthly things (Col 3: 1 – 2).

Our hearts beat in the middle of our chests and, figuratively, in the middle of our being. Your heart is the seat of your emotions and affections. It is where we feel and exist.

Paul instructs the Colossian believers to set their hearts on 'things above', on the 'realities of Heaven' (NLT). To align their very core, even their deepest emotions and desires towards the living God and His rule and reign.

Jesus once said, "Anyone who loves their father or mother more than me is not worthy of me; anyone who loves their son or daughter more than me is not worthy of me'" (Matt 10: 37), a natural extension to, 'Hear, O Israel: The Lord our God, the Lord is one. You shall love the Lord your God with all your heart and with all your soul and with all your might' (Deut 6: 4 – 5). Challenging words.

The truth is, God is not looking for robots. He has always sought relationship. He doesn't need it, but He wants it. He is looking for a people who will choose to be His people. He is looking for people who will love Him.

God also wants our minds set on things above. Our minds are the place where we think and calculate and plan. We love things in our hearts, but we make choices in our minds. A strong will can direct a person towards God or against Him. Paul is imploring the Colossians to use the strength of their will, their intellectual capacity, and their freedom to make right choices, to align their decisions with the purposes of Heaven.

Why? Because as a redeemed people, we now exist in the presence of God and for the purposes of God.

Christ is seated at the right hand of His Father in heaven and we are raised up with Him. We find a similar verse in Eph 2: 6 – 7, 'God raised us up with Christ and seated us with him in the heavenly realms in Christ Jesus, in order that in the coming ages he might show the incomparable riches of his grace, expressed in his kindness to us in Christ Jesus.'

Our spirits were elevated from death and the wrath of God to mercy, forgiveness and a wide, open door to the highest throne. Paul is, in effect, saying, 'you have been given the greatest gift in the known history of the universe – relationship with God, so let your hearts be captivated by it'. Let your hearts desire the same things that God wants and let your minds embrace His will, His thinking and His worldview. Obey Him. Choose what God would choose.

We are already raised up with Christ, so let us intentionally lift our hearts and our minds to the same realm on a daily basis. We can't ignore the Earth, there are still many there in need of a saviour, but we can guard ourselves from being captivated by it.

Suggested prayer: Lord, it is so easy to develop an unhealthy focus on the things of the world. To submit to worry, temptation, distraction and fear. But Lord, I am a citizen of Heaven and I want to love the things that you love and choose the things you choose. Lord, I lift my mind and heart to you today. Amen.

DAY 57

Intercessors

'God shapes the world by prayer. The more praying there is in the world the better the world will be, the mightier the forces against evil' - Mother Teresa.

Let's ask some questions about human beings. First, who are we?

'What is mankind that you are mindful of them,
human beings that you care for them?
You have made them a little lower than the angels
and crowned them with glory and honour.
You made them *rulers* (you have 'given them dominion') over the works of your hands;
you put everything under their feet' (Ps 8: 4 – 6).

The Word, 'rulers' speaks of being God's representative. As humans, we are called to represent God to the rest of Creation and to each other. Who are we? - We are representatives of God.

Second, what power do we have?

'Elijah was a human being, even as we are. He prayed earnestly that it would not rain, and it did not rain on the land for three and a half years. Again, he prayed, and the heavens gave rain, and the earth produced its crops' (James 5: 17).

'The earnest prayer of a righteous person has great power and produces wonderful results' (James 5: 16 NLT). James is not talking about a self-righteous person, but one who has exchanged his/her sin with Christ's righteousness. In short, when we pray, we not only have the same power as Elijah, but the same power as Jesus.

And finally, what authority do we possess?

Let's start with noting the authority Jesus had. A deaf man's ears suddenly started working as Jesus commanded them to 'be opened'. Demons fled at His command and the crashing waters and high winds of a frightening storm were quelled in a moment as Jesus spoke these simple words: 'be still.'

According to Paul, we, who are believers in Jesus, are positioned in the same place of authority as the risen Christ. 'God raised us up with Christ the exalted One, and we ascended with him into the glorious perfection and authority of the heavenly realm, for we are now co-seated as one with Christ' (Eph 2: 6 Passion translation)

No wonder Jesus could say, 'my Father will give you whatever you ask in *my name*' (John 16: 23)

Let's bring all of this together. Have you ever thought about the mystery of the Incarnation? God sent His son (who 'made himself nothing') to become human. He wrote His Word through human beings. He gave the responsibility of taking His good news to the world to believers down the centuries and He has chosen to change the world through us.

So, He calls us to be intercessors in order to do that job. That is who we are, we have His power and His authority.

'God chose, from the time of creation, to work on the earth through humans, not independent of them. He always has and always will, even at the cost of becoming one. Though God is sovereign and all-powerful, Scripture clearly tells us that He has limited Himself, concerning the affairs of earth, to working through human beings' *Intercessory Prayer*, Dutch Sheets

Who are you interceding for?

Suggested prayer: Think about the authority and power you have as a follower and believer in Christ. Then ask God to show you people He wants you to intercede for. Remember that you pray from them in His name. Commit to praying regularly for them and then watch what God can do with simple prayers of faith.

DAY 58

The Best Way to Memorise Scripture

I have always found James 1: 22 – 24 a bit puzzling.

Here's how it reads: 'Do not merely listen to the word, and so deceive yourselves. Do what it says. Anyone who listens to the word but does not do what it says is like someone who looks at his face in a mirror and, after looking at himself, goes away and immediately forgets what he looks like.'

Why would anybody forget what they look like? What does it have to do with obeying the Word of God? And why are we deceiving ourselves if we listen to the Word?

You know how you can read something many times over many years, until one day you see it differently? This happened to me recently when I was reading these verses.

If you are a Christian, you probably already know this, but here's what I saw: If we *only* listen to the message of God's word, but fail to act on it, we can't, in all honestly, say that we have taken it on board. For example, If I agree with the writer of Hebrews that we must share with others (Heb 13: 16) but I then choose not to do so when a brother is in need, can I, with integrity say I have welcomed God's Word into my heart? If I believe I am a good Christian with good theology, but leave my brother in trouble, I have surely deceived myself? I am not a good Christian at all.

The idea of a person looking into a mirror and then forgetting what he looks like is ridiculous. People either admire what they see or wish they looked differently, but nobody forgets his own face.

I think James is saying that it is equally crazy to read something from the Bible, a story or an instruction and then forget it when you have a chance to put it into action. If we are honest with ourselves, it is more likely that I have just *chosen* not to put it into action. If that is the case, can I honestly say I am a faithful follower of Jesus? If I love God's Word, can I pick and choose what I want to obey?

However, an interesting thing happens when we do obey Scripture, especially if there is a cost, and especially if God allows us to see the fruit that results from that act of obedience. We *experience* Scripture. We move from head knowledge to action, and those few verses become a part of us because we have lived them. We have acted on God's words and we are less likely to forget them in the future.

I am not very good at remembering things, but it struck me that here's a great way of memorising Scripture: obey it! Do it!

Suggested prayer: Lord, I don't want to just be a reader of your Word; I want to be a doer. Lord, grant me the courage to take what I read and put it into action. Even if it seems like a hard word to obey, please help me to fix my will towards doing what it says and trusting you for the result. Amen.

DAY 59

How Great is Your God?

When was the last time you read Psalm 139?

At first sight this appears to be a psalm about a person – David. We then personalise it to apply it to ourselves. The word 'I' is used 18 times, the word 'me' 16 times and 'my' is used 11 times.

But I think it is about the greatness of God.

So, let me ask you – How great is *your* God? I'm not asking how great He actually is, but when the chips are down, when the pressures of life kick in, how great do you perceive Him to be?

Let's be honest. We can sing the songs, wonder about how he made the universe, come to church, talk the talk and walk the walk. But what happens when a bill comes in that we can't pay, or someone upsets you? How do we cope when something negative happens at church or work or in the family? How do I avoid a meltdown when things in my life just start going wrong?

How great is my God then?

The overwhelming sense of Psalm 139 is that our Father in Heaven knows us and is with us. David is just reminding himself of that fact. 'You perceive my thoughts from afar' (v 2); 'you are familiar with all my ways' (v 3); 'before a word is on my tongue you know it completely, O Lord' (v 4). That is a great place to start. God is so great; He knows everything about me.

David then marvels at the thought that he could fly like an eagle in the heavens or swim like a fish to the bottom of the ocean and God would still be with him (v 7 – 8). God is so present everywhere that nothing could separate David from His loving care. Even if David were to be completely surrounded by evil, the darkness could never hide him (v 11 – 12). God is so great that His guidance and protection for David knows no bounds. No geographical location or evil presence can keep Him away.

And if God created David in the first place ('you knit me together in my mother's womb' - v 13; 'I was woven together in the depths of the earth' – v 15), then David can trust God's ability to shape and guard his future: 'All the days ordained for me were written in your book before one of them came to be' (v 16).

No wonder he struggles to comprehend the enormity of God's ability to look after every aspect of his life.

>'How precious concerning me are your thoughts, God!
>How vast is the sum of them!
>Were I to count them,
>they would outnumber the grains of sand' (Ps 139: 17 – 18)

When you start trying to imagine the number of grains of sand on the planet and we use words like 'vast', perhaps then we begin to see how great our God is.

Suggested prayer: Go back over Psalm 139 again and pray the words back to God. Apply David's thoughts to your own life and allow the Holy Spirit to stir your own response of thanks, praise and worship to the one who created you. Don't rush this but stay in the moment as you look again at how great God is.

DAY 60

A People Who Bless

In Genesis 12:2 – 3 we eavesdrop on God's call to Abraham. He is about to leave his native country to go to another land, and his descendants will become a great nation. God said to him, 'I will bless you and make you famous, and you will be a blessing to others… All the families on earth will be blessed through you' (NLT).

That's quite a promise. *All* families on earth will be blessed through Abraham. This prophecy was, of course, fulfilled in a major way when Jesus walked the earth. Jesus loved people, gave hope to them, spoke to them about the Father and then died on a cross so that all who believed in Him might receive forgiveness for their sins. He then rose from the dead.

Someone once said, 'the Son of God kissed the earth with heaven's love'. I like that! Jesus brought the blessing of God to earth – the blessing first promised to Abraham: 'All the families on earth will be blessed through you' (NLT).

Blessings multiplied from there. Since Jesus' death, resurrection and ascension, and during the last 2,000 years, many have come to faith in God through Jesus. The Bible calls us 'The Church'. We have received forgiveness, kindness, peace, hope and much more from a God who loves us. We have been blessed. The church is full of people who have been blessed.

So, what is the purpose of the church? Why do we still exist here on Earth rather than just going straight to Heaven? Perhaps one answer is simply this: We are here to bless the Earth around us- *to* kiss the earth with heaven's love. To continue to bring the blessings of God to our friends, families, our communities; to a world that is in desperate need.

How might we do that? Simple: Every morning before your day begins, start the day by praying something like, 'Lord, show me someone I can bless today; show me something I can do to make someone's life better'.

What sort of things can we do? Here's a few ideas:

- Ask a person how they are
- Ask them how their day is going
- Br friendly
- Compliment someone; tell them something you appreciate about them
- Be positive, smile, spread joy, spread laughter
- Be a listening ear; a shoulder to cry on
- Offer to help with something
- Do an unexpected act of kindness; or give a gift
- Send an encouraging text to someone; or Facebook message; or a card or a letter
- Tell someone about Jesus
- Offer to pray from them

Here's a thought: let's start a movement through kindness, laughter and love.

Let's start a blessing movement and then stand back and see what God does with it.

Suggested prayer: Lord, I want to be a person who regularly blesses others, to be a solution instead of a problem, to spread joy, love and life. Lord, show me someone I can bless today; show me something I can do to make someone's life better. Amen.

DAY 61

Two Incarnations

The Incarnation is central to the whole of the New Testament.

The New Testament writers were passionately keen to convey the message that God had visited planet Earth in a unique and special way, but not by way of just a friendly call. The God of the Old Testament had actually *entered* humanity. A baby was placed inside a young teenage girl, a divine being who had 'made himself nothing' (Phil 2: 7) and become human.

Jesus' contemporaries struggled with the idea, of course, that Jesus could be any more than a travelling preacher, at worse a fake messiah, a confidence trickster intent on usurping their fragile authority. They strongly resented His claim that he and His Father in Heaven could be 'one' (John 10: 30). They could not accept His 'wisdom', and they had no idea what to do with the reports of His miracles (Matt 13: 55).

2,000 years later and today, many still wrestle with the notion that God could somehow have become a living, breathing and vulnerable person. If Jesus was the Lord in human form, then, surely, God is no longer perfect, they say. How could the almighty feel physical pain, fear, and how could he have experienced hunger and thirst? Surely, the very idea denies His divinity.

The wonder of the Incarnation, though, is not so much God's ability to become human whilst retaining His nature as God, it's that He would choose to do so! That Jesus would love us that much and go to such lengths to bring us the Father (Heb 10: 19 – 20). It is His humility and deep love for us that really explodes the mind.

When we consider the Scriptures, the Bible itself is another example of an Incarnation. This time God chose to reveal Himself through human vessels - human authors. This is also mind-blowing!

Some might throw arguments at the Bible claiming that isn't perfect in the way *they* think God *should* have written it. There is not enough detailed science in Genesis, they say; some believe they have found contradictions in both the Old and the New Testaments.

But what if the New Testament writers wrote each gospel and letter (to the best of their ability and limited vocabulary), and they contain everything God wanted them to say? - which is (in simple terms): 'I love you; I am not a distant God, I have come to planet Earth, so I know what suffering is like and, in my death and resurrection, I have provided a way for you to have a permanent relationship with me?'

In other words, when the Scriptures were written, what if God was *not* trying to create a document designed to be analysed, torn apart and scrutinised with every microscope possible? What if instead, he was simply using humans to convey a powerful story?

To some, both Incarnations are a stumbling block. However, to those who believe, both incarnations stir us to see, worship and wonder that the perfect God would choose to make Himself known to us, come to us as a human baby, allow Himself to be killed by humans he had created and then even use humans to speak His message to the generations that followed.

God uses humans to speak His message today if you are willing.

Suggested prayer: Lord, thank you that just as Jesus is the incarnate God in human form, perfect in every way, so your Word is the divinely inspired Voice of God perfectly created for the church down the generations and for us today. Lord, give me ears to hear everything you want to say to me. Amen.

DAY 62

The Trinity Verses

I love the fact that God is Himself a community.

The Father, Son and Holy Spirit enjoy a perfect love relationship that defies human understanding and sets the foundation for everything we know and experience in Him.

In the New Testament we first see it in the announcement to Mary of a child she will bear, despite never being 'with a man'. "How will this be," Mary asked the angel, "since I am a virgin?" The angel answered, "The Holy Spirit will come on you, and the power of the Most High will overshadow you. So, the holy one to be born will be called the Son of God.' (Luke 1: 34 – 35)

The Father commands, the Spirit carries out the work and the Son becomes a human being.

A child is born. He is named Jesus and the Son of God as a human person walks the earth in relative obscurity until the time is right to begin His work. But first, a sort of Heavenly commissioning takes place, and the community of God is seen again. 'When all the people were being baptized, Jesus was baptized too. And as he was praying, heaven was opened, and the Holy Spirit descended on Him in bodily form like a dove. And a voice came from heaven: "You are my Son, whom I love; with you I am well pleased."' (Luke 3: 21 – 22)

Jesus healed many and turned towns and villages upside down with His teaching, but He knew when the end was coming for Him, so He promised a new era of the presence of God among humans: 'All this I have spoken while still with you. But the advocate, the Holy Spirit, whom the Father will send in my name, will teach you all things and will remind you of everything I have said to you.' (John 14: 25 – 26)

Our saviour died and rose again, and then ascended to the right hand of His Father in Heaven. Just before leaving, He gave clear instructions to His followers: "All authority in heaven and on earth has been given to me. Therefore, go and make disciples of all nations, baptizing them in the name of the Father and of the Son and of the Holy Spirit…" (Matt 28: 18 – 19).

The disciples and new believers subsequently spread the good news of the Son risen from the dead. They baptized in the name of all three members of the Godhead and The Lord began forming a new community – a human community of His presence. 'And in him you too are being built together to become a dwelling in which God lives by his Spirit.' (Eph 2: 22).

The Father continued to pour out His revelation of truth and Heaven's resources through the Spirit as believers down the ages worshipped the Son and followed His teaching and example. Like Paul, they kept asking that God, the father of Jesus, may give them the Spirit of wisdom and revelation, (Eph 1: 17).

And God was always faithful to answer: 'Because you are his sons, God sent the Spirit of his Son into our hearts, the Spirit who calls out, "Abba, Father."' (Gal 4: 6).

It strikes me that the Trinity is far more than a theological concept. It is central to every aspect of the Gospel story. The community of God has come to Earth and created a family of which you and I are invited to be part of. Perfect communion, along with knowledge, wisdom and love is on display in the Godhead and they want to share it with each one of us.

Suggested prayer: Take a moment to worship the one true God, an eternal Being existent as Father, Son and Holy Spirit. We may never understand all the theology, but we can express our wonder, love and gratitude to the One who has revealed Himself to us through His creation, His Word and the death and resurrection of Jesus.

DAY 63

You Give Them Something to Eat

Years ago, my wife and I ran out of money. We had nothing left to buy food with and I remember walking into my kitchen calling out to God. 'You promised to provide all of our needs', before standing in silence, not knowing what to do.

Within two minutes of my prayer the doorbell rang and, as I opened the door, a letter was thrust into my hand. 'This was delivered to my house; I think it is yours.' The money in the envelope was enough to re-stock our kitchen cupboards. Did I just experience God doing a miracle? To this day, I believe I did.

Sometime later, I came across this statement from Jesus: 'I tell you, whoever believes in me will do the works I have been doing, and they will do even greater things than these, because I am going to the Father' (John 14: 12). Is it possible we can do miracles too?

At another time, Jesus and His disciples were in a remote place. Jesus had been teaching a large crowd and, after some time had elapsed, the disciples became quite concerned for the peoples' welfare. 'They haven't had a meal in a while, send them away Lord, so they can buy something to eat' (Mark 6: 36).

But Jesus had another plan and you'll be familiar, I'm sure, with His subsequent miracle: the feeding of the five thousand with just a small amount of food. What's easy to miss though is Jesus' initial response to His disciples' concerns even before he even takes hold of the five loaves and two fish. He says to them, 'You give them something to eat!' (Mark 6: 37)

The twelve disciples had just returned from mission where, by faith in Jesus, they had preached the kingdom of God, cast out demons and laid hands on sick people, seeing many miraculously healed. They had experienced first-hand the joy and privilege of God touching lives through them. Now they are faced with another impossible task, Jesus seems to be saying to them,

'OK, you've healed the sick in my name, surely you can multiply a few pieces of bread and fish?'

Needless to say, they didn't understand what He was saying to them and by the time their mental calculators had worked out that eight months of an average wage would be needed to buy that amount of food, Jesus had already decided what He was going to do.

But how Jesus multiplies the food is fascinating. It is almost like He is saying, 'listen boys, watch closely, this is how you do a miracle (with the Holy Spirit's help, of course!).' Maybe, 2,000 years later, He is teaching us too.

- He asked the disciples what they had. They brought Him a few small loaves and fish. It wasn't much, but it was something. Applying this to you and me today, what miracle are *you* asking God for? So, what have you got in front of you however small, that you can start with?

- Jesus made some plans. He arranged the people into groups of hundreds and fifties. Even with those numbers Jesus was expecting a miracle. Use your imagination, soaked in prayer, to start planning what you might do with what you have.

- He then looked up to Heaven. I love the way Jesus models dependence for us – dependence on the Father's will and the power of the Holy Spirit. Take the opportunity to gaze upon the King and seek His leading.

- Finally, Jesus took action. He gave thanks, broke the bread and gave it to the disciples to distribute.

I wonder how many times we have pleaded with God to do something when all along He was whispering 'You've got this! You give them something to eat.'

Suggested prayer: Do you have a need or an ongoing prayer that you feel God hasn't answered yet? Prayerfully ask the Lord if there is something He wants you to do. Ask Him to show you what is in front of you, however small, that you might start with. Then pray for His leading as to the plans to make from there.

DAY 64

I Will Give You Rest

I'm not very good at winding down.

Something in my head tells me that to honour God, I should work hard every day, do long hours, not be a slacker, persevere through the headaches and tick lots of things on my to-do list. Then, when I've hacked away at that for a good, solid number of hours, I figure it might be ok to take some time off.

No wonder I feel tired all the time.

The Bible mentions 'rest' in some odd places. One is in Exodus 33. Earlier in the book, Moses had spent 40 days in the presence of God; now in chapter 33 and back among the general population, he would regularly walk away from the camp and enter the 'tent of meeting,' where he and the Lord would speak face-to-face. Moses was the only one on the planet who knew what it was to encounter the living God at close quarters and survive.

We have a record of what took place in one such meeting. If we could have crept in part way through the conversation, we would have heard Moses say, '…If you are pleased with me, teach me your ways so I may know you and continue to find favour with you…' (Ex 33: 13 NIV). Curiously, the Lord replies with 'My Presence will go with you, and I will give you rest.' Why rest?

Moses had asked for a greater understanding of God's ways, for a deeper knowledge of Him and for continued, ongoing favor. God responded with, 'I'll give you rest.'

I frequently find myself not knowing what to do in life and in ministry. It might be a decision that needs to be made or a difficult email to respond to. I think I've prayed more as a pastor than I ever did before. It is almost a daily routine to ask God, yet again, 'please give me wisdom'.

Moses also seemed desperate to be equipped for ministry: 'teach me', he cries, 'teach me your ways. I need information, training, mentoring. That way, God, I'll know you better and find favor with you.'

But God seems to be saying, 'Welcome to my presence, that's all you need for now. Rest from your strivings'.

I am grateful for all the training and mentoring I've had, for the books and people that have crossed my path and for the fruit of study and hard work, but I think sometimes God simply says, 'my presence is enough for you. Stop. Just stop.'

'Enter my presence and stay there. When it is time to move, go on my instruction and then my presence will go with you. That way you will rest from attempting tasks in your own strength and you will see the Lord do wonderful things'

'My Presence will go with you, and I will give you rest.'

Suggested prayer: Take time out today to slow down, stop and come consciously into the Lord's presence. He is with you, always, of course, but sometimes we need to rest from our activities, be aware of Him and switch off from all the distractions around us. Have an open Bible with you and a humble heart. Try to do this every day.

DAY 65

Talking to Myself

Who is he talking to? It sounds like he is talking to himself!

Psalm 103, starts off with a short phrase that is often repeated in other Psalms: 'Praise the Lord, my soul.' The author says it again in verse 2, 'Praise the Lord, my soul.' And again, at the end of the psalm.

King David, who wrote these words, also wrote Psalm 57 and there is similar language here: 'Awake, my soul! Awake, harp and lyre! I will awaken the dawn' (57: 8). David is telling himself to wake up and give glory to God.

He's talking to himself.

My wife and I were chatting recently about how different people are and how those differences can often boil down to personality type – just one way that God has made each of us unique. However, we are also part of a fallen human race and in the process of being renewed. Not everything that makes me, me, is necessarily as God intended. We all have a mixture of positive attributes in our personalities and negative ones that are yet to be transformed.

For example, some of us will naturally have a more positive outlook than others. Others, not so. My personality type is melancholic which, according to some studies describes someone who is analytical (yep, that's true), task orientated (tick), self-motivated (yes), a perfectionist (oh dear), but can be quite shy and 'deep'; and with a tendency to want to hide away occasionally. Actually, for some, discouragement, even depression is part of the story and can hit hard. But, hey, we can be really creative!

Without Christ, I would quite easily see the negative in most situations, but when I read the Bible, I don't think I am alone. Look at the way David expresses himself in Psalm 13:

> "How long, Lord? Will you forget me forever?
> How long will you hide your face from me?

> How long must I wrestle with my thoughts
> and day after day have sorrow in my heart" (Psalm 13: 1 – 2)

When we read David's soul-bearing poetry, some of it makes me wonder if he might have been a melancholic too. We can't be sure of course but, if that is true, then he has got something important to say in this space: talk to yourself! When discouragement sets in, when there's sorrow in your heart, speak to your soul!

Our souls are fragile. We were once spiritually dead in our sins, but through Christ's death on the cross and resurrection we have been 'made alive' (Eph 2: 1, 5). Now we are on the path of transformation, but we are still subject to temptation, discouragement, and spiritual attack.

For every Christian, there are times when we are tempted to dwell on the negative – and every personality type has a bad day. Perhaps those are the moments God would have us look in the mirror and talk to our inner selves: "Awake! Come on! Today is a new day and we are going to praise God and trust Him!"

Suggested prayer: The next time you find a moment to pray, speak to your soul first. Tell your soul to praise God and worship Him. Tell your soul to express faith in God and put your trust in Him. Like David, make a decision to praise and trust, even when it is the last thing you feel like doing.

DAY 66

Reach out a Hand

In Mark 5 we read the remarkable story of the woman who crept up behind Jesus, squeezing through the crowd until she could touch the hem of His robe. Having suffered for years with a bleeding condition, she thought to herself, "If I just touch his clothes, I'll be healed". And she was!

Mark seems to suggest that Jesus didn't even know what had happened until after 'power had gone out from him' (Mark 5: 30). What gave this lady such extraordinary faith? She hadn't asked for healing, Jesus had given her no promises; in fact, it looks like Jesus didn't even know she existed until she received her healing.

Mark tells us that it was after she had 'heard about Jesus' that she came to Him. Her faith simply came from that: what she had heard about Jesus.

Perhaps that is helpful to us in our time of need. When we are looking to God for a solution, trying to remember a promise in Scripture we can cling to, what have we simply heard about Jesus that can help us in this moment?

For starters, we know He loves us, that He died on a cross for us. Then we have the stories of Jesus in the gospels: we see His compassion for the lost and hurting, we witness His authority over sickness and death, the miracles of walking on water and calming a powerful storm.

And, of course, we have our own stories of how Jesus has been faithful to us in our journey with Him to this point. A time, perhaps, when you knew His guidance or His peace. A moment when a particular verse of Scripture was just what you needed.

Looking more broadly there are the many testimonies of brothers and sisters around the world who have experienced the transforming power of God, through Jesus Christ. Like the prophet Habakkuk, we can pray, 'Lord, I have heard of your fame; I stand in awe of your deeds, Lord. Repeat them in our day, in our time make them known' (Hab 3: 2).

Sometimes, just on the basis of what we have heard about Jesus, all we need to do is just reach out a hand to Him and see what He will do. Jesus said, 'Which of you, if your son asks for bread, will give him a stone? Or if he asks for a fish, will give him a snake? If you, then, though you are evil, know how to give good gifts to your children, how much more will your Father in heaven give good gifts to those who ask him!' (Matt 7: 9 – 11).

The Bible seems to suggest that anybody can have extraordinary faith, because a mustard seed is all we need. Perhaps it starts with remembering what we have heard about Jesus; then all we have to do is simply reach out a hand asking Him for help.

Suggested prayer: Next time you are asking God for something, remind yourself of the stories of Jesus. The things He did and said. Remind yourself of His faithfulness to you, what He has done for you. Speak out prayers of thanks for those things, naming them one after the other. Then picture yourself reaching out and touching the hem of his cloak as you bring your request to Him.

DAY 67

The 'One Another' Scriptures

How might we help each other to grow in God?

I'm glad you asked!

One way is to practice the 'One Another Scriptures'. There are lots of them scattered throughout the New Testament. Although they all are simple and easy to do, they are also life-transforming. Here are a few to kick us off – all from the book of Romans.

- 'Love one another warmly as Christians and be eager to show respect for one another' (12: 10).

- 'Aim at those things that bring peace and that help strengthen one another' (14: 19).

- 'Accept one another' (15: 7).

If we bind these together, we create a rich tapestry of peace, acceptance, strength and respect, all stitched together with love. Imagine your church or Christian organisation soaked in these values!

Someone might ask: *how* might I show love or *how* might I bring peace? What are the practical implications? A few more 'One Another' Scriptures may help:

- 'Agree with one another' (2 Cor 13: 11).

- 'Show your love by being tolerant with one another' (Eph 4: 2).

- 'Be kind and tender-hearted to one another and forgive one another' (Eph 4: 32).

Do those exhortations seem too hard? If they do, think about them as buried treasure. I love stories of ancient explorers trying to find hidden riches. They risk everything, but the sweat is worth it. These verses are like precious jewels. A little work to discover them and use them can yield mighty rewards.

For example, how can we be tolerant with each other? Maybe by searching for the best in those around us rather than focusing on the differences. Perhaps one way of showing love is to steer the ship towards kindness, being eager to forgive. How about pursuing peace by seeking common ground before jumping too quickly into disagreement?

The next two might seem contradictory at first.

- 'Submit yourselves to one another' (Eph 5: 21).
- 'Teach and instruct one another with all wisdom' (Col 3: 16).

How can I instruct or teach someone and yet submit myself to them at the same time - surely a teacher or instructor is a person in authority?

Perhaps look at it this way: If we have an opportunity to teach someone, let's do it with the wisdom only God can give. How do we find that wisdom? We humble ourselves and ask God for it. We rely on Him to do the job through us. We therefore teach with humility too - we submit our gifts rather than force them.

And lastly…

- Above everything, love one another earnestly, because love covers over many sins (1 Pet 4: 8).

The most popular 'one another' statement in the Bible is by far the command to love one another (it occurs over 15 times). All the others seem to point to it and underline it with great passion. Love each other *earnestly*.

Suggested prayer: Which of these 'one-another' Scriptures has spoken to you the most? Has the Holy Spirit challenged you to practice one of them on anyone in particular? Pray for God to help you rise up to the challenge and obey His Word.

DAY 68

The Unforgivable Sin

Ok, so let's tackle this one!

An often talked about (and, sadly, joked about) topic. A few thoughts.

I wonder if you have ever felt you've done something that not even God can forgive. Maybe you expressed anger towards God, or you took His name in vain; perhaps you stopped following Him for a season; or you might have done something so terrible in your mind that you will never be able to forgive yourself for it. How can God want anything to do with you after that?

Jesus talked about a sin that would never be forgiven – the blasphemy of the Holy Spirit. Have you committed it?

Well, the good news is if you are reading this, you probably haven't!

The other good news is the Bible promises in a letter written by one of the disciples closest to Jesus: 'If we confess our sins, he is faithful and just and will forgive us our sins and purify us from all unrighteousness' (1 John1: 9). God forgives. God is a forgiving God – even if we don't always forgive ourselves.

When Jesus talked about the unforgivable sin in Mark 3: 28 - 29 (whoever blasphemes against the Holy Spirit will never be forgiven; they are guilty of an eternal sin), he was addressing teachers of the law who had witnessed amazing miracles performed by Jesus' own hand. Jesus had clearly demonstrated His authority over evil, He had healed the sick and He had expounded the Scriptures with breath-taking authority. But rather than rejoicing in what they saw and heard, the teachers of the law accused Him of having a demon; even worse, being the devil himself.

To us who are believers centuries later, Jesus could be no-one else but the long-awaited Messiah, the man from heaven, but His critics failed to see that the spirit working through him was the same as the Holy Spirit of God. God's Son was right in front of them, but they did not recognise Him.

And so, Jesus warned them that the most serious thing was to attribute to the devil what God is in fact doing – sending His Son to Earth and shining a light in the darkness. Because Jesus wasn't the Messiah they were waiting for, it was easier for them to write Him off as evil.

So, what is the unforgivable sin? I believe It is to reach the end of your life and still fail to recognise who Jesus is and therefore not take steps to respond to His call upon your life.

The good news is that some did eventually believe in Jesus and become followers. As long as we have breath in our lungs it is never too late to make that course change.

Suggested prayer: Think of people in your life who have not yet recognised Jesus as God's Son or sensed His call upon their lives. Pray that God will bring them to the place of receiving His love and forgiveness.

DAY 69

Unless the Lord Builds the House

I often find myself drawn to Psalm 127, particularly it's opening phrase, 'Unless the Lord builds the house, the builders labour in vain.'

This, of course, was reflected in Jesus' response to Peter's magnificent declaration of His divine identity ('you are the Christ, the son of the living God') when Jesus included in His reply the words, 'I will build my church' (Matt 16: 18). God the Father, Son and Holy Spirit are together architect and site manager of the world's greatest building project and, although we are sons and daughters, we are servants too – we are serving His purposes. How easy it is to forget that!

I think that's why the psalmist has included a verse which basically says, 'why are you burning the candle at both ends, driving yourself to a nervous breakdown, when all I'm calling you to do is some manageable tasks each day, under the guidance of the Holy Spirit, which will give you plenty of time to catch enough sleep and rest ready for the next day?'

> "In vain you rise early
> sand stay up late,
> toiling for food to eat—
> for he grants sleep to those he loves." (Ps 127: 2)

I was at a meeting recently, where a young lady shared something of what she felt God was saying to her through a season she was going through. The word from God was simply, 'you rest, I work!'

However, I have often been confused by the rest of the psalm, verses 3 – 5. Here we seem to move off topic and on to the blessings of children both randomly and suddenly. What has this got to do with building God's house?

The solution may lie in the next psalm, number 128. Many people read it alongside Ps 127.

The first verse of Ps 128 immediately encourages us to 'fear the Lord' and 'walk in his ways'. We might say, remember who is in charge – He's the architect and site manager. Follow His commands and do the things He has called you to do. Then (v 2), you will see the fruit of your labour, but you will see it in two places.

First, God's building and city will grow and flourish, according to His plans – 'may you see the prosperity of Jerusalem' (v 5). The one who builds the house (and watches over the city – see 127: 1) wants his children to experience the joy of a job well done in partnership with Him. But that's not all.

The rest of the psalm describes a family blessed by the Lord. The Psalmists wife is a fruitful vine, sons or children are like olive shoots, fresh and full of hope. As we build His way, in His timescale and in His strength, not relying on our own energy or motivated by our own agendas, then even our homes are blessed.

Suggested prayer: Lord, please help me to remember that you are the one building the house – your Kingdom here on Earth. Lord, I want to find the right balance between working hard for you and resting in trust that you can do far more than anything I can achieve on my own. Lord, help me to discern the difference between the things I want to do and the things you have called me to do. Amen.

DAY 70

Trembling before God's Word

Have you ever heard a Bible story so many times, becoming so familiar with it that it no longer impacts you? I think that happens with the parable of the four soils (Matt 13: 1 – 23) – at least it does to me!

Some of us subconsciously think to ourselves: Everyone knows Jesus is talking about the Gospel – some people don't want to know the Gospel and Satan takes away the Word; some do want to know, but their commitment is shallow, and they easily fall away; some respond positively to the Gospel but, in time, temptations and the pressures of life make them ineffective. Finally, some jump in with both feet and obey God's Word. They put Him first in their lives and become very fruitful.

Job done, right? If you are a Christian reading this, you hope that you are soil number four and you feel sad for the other poor saps who are in one of the other three categories.

But I would like to suggest there is much more going on here: I think this is a parable for all people, including and especially Christians. Jesus is directing this towards everyone who might follow Him, and he is asking: how much do we allow the *whole* of the Word of God to change us?

Jesus makes it very clear that the 'seed' in the story is God's Word, which would include His teaching, teaching that was varied, from instructions about money, prayer and marriage, to challenges about priorities, righteousness and love for one another. With the parable of the soils, he is, in effect, asking: How much will you allow my words to take root in your life?

For example, if we try to ignore His words about forgiveness, is it possible that we are actually allowing Satan to take those words away like the description of the first soil? Or, if we start to allow career or family or even ministry to become more important than our relationship and obedience to God, then are we any better than the person described in soil number three?

No wonder Jesus said, "if you don't understand this parable how will you understand any parable?" (Mark 4: 13).

Which leads us to ask: how seriously do we take God's Word? We can nod our heads during a sermon and sign statements of faith, but do we embrace the pain of obeying it? Especially the hard bits.

Isaiah 66: 2 describes the believer as one who, 'trembles at my word'. That is a powerful phrase. Think about that for a moment. A child of God is one who handles the Scriptures with deep, almost fearful reverence.

Trembling before God's Word might mean wrestling with some of those 'difficult' verses we find in the Bible, knowing that as we do so God can use them to bring transformation to our lives. Even as Bible-believing Christians we can choose to be hard soil, ignoring His Word; or shallow soil, with no real commitment to it; or even crowded soil with mixed priorities. But we can also choose to tremble before His Word, eager to feed on it and hungry enough for it to change us.

Suggested prayer: Lord, I don't want to just honor your Word with my thoughts or my lips, but with my actions. With my obedience. Lord, please put in my heart a deep reverence for your Word. I want to be a person who is hungry, eager to feed on your laws, stories and promises and committed to obeying it. Amen.

DAY 71

Carrying Burdens

There is a small section in Paul's letter to the Galatians, which at first reading, appears to be contradictory.

In chapter 6: 5, Paul instructs each believer to 'carry his own load', but earlier, in verse 2 he has already told them to 'carry each other's burdens'. What is going on here?

Let' start with a small quiz – try to be honest!

1. If you have a need, or are going through a difficult time, who do you share it with?
    a. No one
    b. Everyone
    c. Close friends only
    d. Close family
    e. Close Christian friends
2. If you see a friend or family member in need or going through a difficult time, do you want to help?
    a. Yes
    b. No
    c. Maybe

I have known many people who answer 'a' for the second question, but also 'a' for the first. They love helping others, but they won't even ask God to intervene in the problem they are going through, let alone ask anyone else! I heard one person say, 'I won't burden God with my problems, He has enough people to worry about!'.

Having said that, we could almost say that answering 'a' to both questions actually fulfills Paul's instructions to the Galatians – 'Don't burden anyone with your problems' (carry your own load) but be the first to help a brother or sister in need (carry each other's burdens).

The trouble is – that doesn't work! If I fail to express my need to others (usually because I am too proud), I deny them the opportunity to share my burdens with me. I deny them the chance to obey God's Word and be a blessing.

So, what's the answer? Verse 1 puts the passage in context. We are talking about restoring someone caught in a sin. So, although we might encourage general help towards one another at any level, primarily we are concerned here with a brother or a sister who has done wrong, with two important provisos: don't get sucked into the sin yourself (v 1) and avoid the temptation to imagine you are any better than the person you are helping. In other words, be humble (v 3).

Being humble is the key here. How do we measure humility? One way is to test our actions (v 4). Not by comparing them to others (where I might feel I fare quite well, especially somebody I am 'helping'!), but by immersing myself in the presence of the Holy Spirit ('live by the Spirit'; 'be led by the Spirit' – Gal 5: 16,18) and asking him 'search my heart' (Ps 139: 23).

Carrying my own load does not mean keeping my needs away from the Lord. Quite the opposite, it means humbling myself, trusting in Him to meet my needs. And if I have learned to be humble, perhaps then I will allow others to help me too.

If you and I have hearts open to the gentle probing of the Holy Spirit, and have hearts that are growing in humility, we will be able to carry each other's burdens (without judgment, if sin is involved), and we will allow others to help us. If we can get this right, imagine what blessings from Heaven might flow!

Suggested prayer: "Lord, please create in me a new heart, a heart that is not too proud or fearful to admit my needs and ask for help. Help me to carry others' burdens without judgment and help me to create in my friendships and community dependence on God and love and care for each other. Amen."

DAY 72

Dealing with Guilt

You know that moment. You shouldn't have said it – you went too far. That decision you made – not your finest hour. Some say that the pricked conscience proves the existence of God. The feeling of guilt tells your heart that you are ultimately accountable to a higher power for your thoughts, words and actions. I'm not sure if Natural Selection can do that.

David lets us in on a personal moment of shame in Psalm 32. This penitential psalm is remarkably candid. Although we don't know the details of the deeds that led to David's feelings of guilt, he is clear that he has sinned, and he has no qualms about taking personal responsibility for what he has done.

In fact, later in v 8 – 9, he counsels the reader to follow his example. 'Do not be like the horse or the mule who are not moved by conscience, but must be compelled by outside forces of discipline, like a bit or bridle.' In other words, 'don't wait for consequences to catch up on you – listen to the feelings of guilt and deal with your sin now. Confess to the Lord!'

Guilt is a powerful emotion and David describes it vividly in terms of both physical and emotional suffering:

> 'When I kept silent,
> my bones wasted away
> through my groaning all day long.
> For day and night
> your hand was heavy on me;
> my strength was sapped
> as in the heat of summer. (Ps 32: 3 – 4)

That is one deflated individual! But then David prayed. He admitted his faults to God; he stopped trying to hide them and he experienced the relief of forgiveness in verse 5:

> Then I acknowledged my sin to you
> and did not cover up my iniquity.
> I said, "I will confess
> my transgressions to the Lord."
> And you forgave the guilt of my sin.

The psalm starts with, 'Blessed is he whose transgressions are covered' (v 1). That tells us that God would rather bless us than hurt us. He would rather forgive us than chastise us. David realises this and with the passion of an evangelist calls out, 'Therefore let all the faithful pray to you while you may be found' (v 6). He even ends the psalm with rejoicing and singing. The forgiven can once again enjoy a glad heart.

Charles Spurgeon once said, "I would bear any affliction rather than be burdened by a guilty conscience." Guilt weighs down; it drains and saps. God made it, but only as a means to restoration. Guilt is not a gift to be held on to or buried. It is a gift to be exchanged for repentance and a new beginning.

Psalm 32 is great news for every human being and its fullness was made possible by Christ's death on the cross. When Jesus died for our sin, we learned *why* God can forgive us forever – His Son paid the ultimate price.

No wonder the New Testament authors cannot help but continue to celebrate David's penitential, yet joyful psalm. James writes, 'Come near to God and he will come near to you. Wash your hands, you sinners, and purify your hearts, you double-minded. Grieve, mourn and wail. Change your laughter to mourning and your joy to gloom. Humble yourselves before the Lord, and he will lift you up' (James 4: 8 – 10).

Suggested prayer: Is God quickening your conscience to confess something to Him today? If guilt has been gently tapping your shoulder for a season, it may be Lord urging you to bring the matter to Him. Remember, God is a God of forgiveness and restoration. Express your repentance to Him and if you have offended another, ask the Lord to show you how to restore that relationship.

DAY 73

Generosity

Eric and his team had been looking forward to this day for some time – a 'fellowship meal' to celebrate another anniversary. He could imagine the tables brimming with creamy pasta dishes, hot casseroles, delicious pies, pizzas and more. And don't even mention the desserts – self-control would be out the window!

The wonderful thing about these events was that all the food came from the people in the community, and even though there was little coordination, the various dishes that turned up on the day were almost always just the right amount of savoury and sweet, bread and salad, meat and dessert for those who would be there. God's regular little miracle.

Except for that particular day.

Mrs. Adler was sick, the Lewis family overslept, Joe and Margie forgot to go shopping yesterday and many portions seemed smaller than normal. The resulting smorgasbord was uninspiring and barely enough.

This was not the problem that Bezalel and Oholiab faced.

Moses had led the Israelites out of Egypt (at which point, surprisingly, the Egyptians gave generously of their possessions) and to the other side of the Red Sea after God split the waters. Moving forward they journeyed to Mount Sinai where the Lord gave Moses the 10 commandments. There, God also gave Moses detailed plans to build a tabernacle – a place where sacrifices would be made to atone for sin and where God would dwell among His people.

Bezalel and Oholiab headed up a large team of craftsmen and women, skilled in metalwork, joinery, perfumery and textiles to construct everything from lampstands to altars to garments for the priests. The raw materials for all these things would come from a freewill offering given by any Israelite wishing to do so.

By the time we reach Exodus chapter 36, the offering is in full swing, but the text tells us that 'morning after morning' the people continued to give. So much so that the craftsman had to put their tools down, find Moses and tell him that the people were bringing a lot more than was needed (Ex 36; 5). The spirit of generosity was so huge that Moses actually had to 'restrain' the Israelites from giving any more.

Imagine that being a problem in your organisation.

Imagine a love offering for a brother in need so large that he can share it with two others. Imagine the call for volunteers to start a new ministry creating such a response that the size of the ministry triples overnight.

Imagine a spirit of generosity so profound that you don't know what to do with all the gifts that have been given.

It is interesting to note the order of things in the building of the tabernacle: God made the plans and He blessed His people with abilities and resources. God shared His plans with His people, who, in turn, used their time, skills and possessions (freely and generously) to carry them out. The result? God filled the tabernacle with His presence and His glory (Ex 40: 34 – 35).

Imagine that happening at your place.

Suggested prayer: Lord, you are a generous God, I want to be generous too. Help me to see all the many and varied ways that you have poured your blessings out on me, so that I will freely and willingly give of my time and resources to others for your Kingdom's sake. Amen.

DAY 74

Purity

I love the word 'lavish'

It is used a few times in the Bible. After Daniel interpreted Nebuchadnezzar's dream, the king lavished him with many gifts (Dan 2: 48); Hosea rebukes Israel for turning to Baal worship even after the Lord had lavished his people with bountiful harvests, silver and gold (Hos 2: 8).

The word 'lavish' speaks of generosity, overflow, many gifts given freely. I believe the Apostle John had no choice but to pick this word as he wrestled with the impossible task of articulating in human terms the greatness and wonder of God's love towards us: 'How great is the love the Father has lavished on us, that we should be called children of God!' (1 John 3: 1).

'And that is what we are!' he continues, not able to stop. The deep truth of being an adopted son/daughter of God, with everything forgiven and God's Grace arriving daily in bucket-loads has hit John like a sledgehammer.

But John still doesn't finish there. In verse two, he starts imagining the future. In effect he says, 'I don't know what our bodies, our lives, are going to look like, but I know that, somehow, we are going to be just like Jesus; in fact, we are going to see Him face-to-face and live with Him. Wow!'

Wow, indeed. But then, in the light of all of this, John suddenly changes tack, adopting a more serious tone.

'Everyone who has this hope in him purifies himself, just as He is pure' (v 3), he writes. In other words, once these truths of adoption have sunk deeply into our souls, they should profoundly affect our hearts and determine how we live – with purity. Just as Jesus lived a pure life.

In what ways did Jesus live a pure life? There are a lot of things we could say, but let's focus on just one here: Everything Jesus did was to glorify the Father.

Jesus never had a selfish thought, and He wasn't driven by the goal of personal success. He didn't get up in the morning hoping to expand his portfolio, increase his influence or grow his YouTube channel. He didn't speak in such a way as to *try* and draw large crowds – he simply spoke the truth, loved the lost and healed the sick, and the crowds came anyway.

'I only do what I see my Father doing' (John 5: 19 – my paraphrase), He said. That's how Jesus lived a pure life. Devoid of selfish motives, Jesus made it His sole aim to please His Father in Heaven.

When I ponder this I realise, if I am honest, how little I consciously do just to please my Father. A lot of what I do is, at least, partly tainted by what *I* would like to achieve today, this year or in life. I have dreams I must go for.

If an honest search of your heart reveals the same, perhaps David's prayer strikes a chord, 'Create in me a pure heart, Oh God' (Ps 51: 10), In other words, 'Lord, create in me a heart whose sole goal is to please my Father in heaven'

Suggested prayer: Lord, create in me a pure heart. Please work in my heart so deeply that my sole aim in life is to please my Father in Heaven. Lord, I want to live for you. Amen.

DAY 75

Peace

I don't know what to do; everything seems to be falling apart.

'Come to me, all you who are weary and burdened, and I will give you rest' (Matt 11: 28).

How do I do that? I don't even know how to find the Lord. Where is He? I can't see Him.

'The Lord is near to all who call on him, to all who call on him in truth' (Ps 145: 18).'

'The Lord is near. Do not be anxious about anything, but in every situation, by prayer and petition, with thanksgiving, present your requests to God. And the peace of God, which transcends all understanding, will guard your hearts and your minds in Christ Jesus' (Phil 4: 5 – 7).

Look, I'm a beginner here. I have no idea where to start.

'When you pray, go into your room, close the door and pray to your Father, who is unseen. Then your Father, who sees what is done in secret, will reward you' (Matt 6: 6).

'Cast all your anxiety on him because he cares for you' (1 Pet 5: 7).

'Be still, and know that I am God' (Ps 46: 10).

How will I know God will hear me?

'You will call on me and come and pray to me, and I will listen to you. You will seek me and find me when you seek me with all your heart' (Jer 29: 12 – 13).

Is the Lord even interested in my prayers? Who am I? I'm nobody special.

'The righteous cry out, and the Lord hears them; he delivers them from all their troubles. The Lord is close to the broken-hearted and saves those who are crushed in spirit' (Ps 34: 17 – 18).

I don't know if I can cope with this storm any longer. How much longer do I have to endure this?

'No discipline seems pleasant at the time, but painful. Later on, however, it produces a harvest of righteousness and peace for those who have been trained by it' (Heb 12: 11).

'You (God) will keep in perfect peace those whose minds are steadfast because they trust in you' (Is 26: 3).

'May the God of hope fill you with all joy and peace as you trust in him, so that you may overflow with hope by the power of the Holy Spirit' (Rom 15: 13).

I would love to receive God's blessing right now, His strength and favour while I endure this storm. Are you sure God wants this for me too?

'"The Lord bless you and keep you;
the Lord make his face shine on you
and be gracious to you;
the Lord turn his face toward you
and give you peace' (Num 6: 24 – 26).

Suggested prayer: Find a time and place every day where you can be alone with your Father in Heaven. Read one or two of the verses of Scripture in today's reading, slowly. Read them to God and allow the words to guide you in your prayers. Take a moment each day to be still, worship Him, and then tell Him about the cares and troubles in your life. Express your faith and trust in Him.

DAY 76

Purpose

Do you have a particular verse that inspires you in the Bible; a 'life-verse'? One that gives you hope, courage or helps you re-focus every time you read it?

Mine is Ephesians 2: 10 - 'we are God's handiwork, created in Christ Jesus to do good works, which God prepared in advance for us to do.'

I love how this verse is presented in the Passion Translation: 'We have become his poetry, a re-created people that will fulfill the destiny he has given each of us, for we are joined to Jesus, the Anointed One. Even before we were born, God planned in advance our destiny and the good works we would do to fulfill it!'

We are God's handiwork, His 'poetry', or 'workmanship' as the NIV used to say. God's creative power is fully displayed in us. God loves to make beauty out of chaos, strength out of brokenness and destiny from an empty life transformed by grace. Wow!

All of it is for purpose. As wonderful as God's free gift of salvation is, I believe it is only the beginning, a down-payment - step one on the road to recovery, and a mere glimpse of the wonders and adventures to come. I love saying to young people, 'the greatest joy in life is discovering the things God has for us to do and then walking in them hand-in-hand with Him'.

King David had a strong sense of God's destiny for him when he wrote of his existence even before his mother gave birth: 'Your eyes saw my unformed body; all the days ordained for me were written in your book before one of them came to be' (Ps 139: 16).

Jeremiah also knew God's call on his life, when the Lord's word came to him, saying: 'Before I formed you in the womb I knew you, and before you were born I set you apart; I appointed you as a prophet to the nations' (Jer 1: 5).

Ephesians 2: 10 follows from several references to predestination at the beginning of the letter. We were chosen 'in Him/Christ' before the creation of the world to be a holy people, blameless even. Motivated by love, God predetermined us to be adopted into His family through faith in Christ, and we were predestined to play a part in his great plan of salvation (Eph 1: 4 – 5, 11 – 12).

No wonder Paul can boast with confidence that God has works for us to do – a wonderful future in Him.

For Jesus, doing the things the Father had called Him to do was as essential as eating regular meals. 'My food is to do the will of Him who sent me and to finish His work' (John 4: 34). What does food give us? Survival, sustenance, healing, joy, pleasure and the difference between life and death.

I don't think Jesus was saying that His big interest in life was to fulfill God's purposes for Him; I don't think He was even saying it was even His greatest passion. I think He was saying that it lay at the core of everything He lived and died for.

That's why Eph 2: 10 is my favourite verse in the whole of the Bible.

Suggested prayer: Lord, thank you that you created me to be your poetry, joined with Jesus by faith, with a destiny to fulfill. Lord, help me to discover each day the things you have called me to do. For your glory, Amen.

DAY 77

The Secret of Joy

In the middle of Paul's first missionary journey, he and Barnabas visited Pisidian Antioch (Acts 13: 14). Paul delivered a blistering sermon in the local synagogue, sweeping his audience through a vast swathe of Israel's history, from Moses to Joshua, Samuel to David and on to Jesus Christ, raised from the dead. Supported by an impressive knowledge of the Hebrew Scriptures, Paul skillfully steered everyone in the room towards the conclusion that salvation can only be found through belief in Jesus for the forgiveness of sins.

Many of the Jews and Gentile converts wanted to hear more and a week later the whole city gathered. But not everyone was happy.

Some 'talked abusively' against them (Acts 13: 45). Undeterred, Paul and Barnabas continued to speak out until 'the word of the Lord spread through the whole region' (Acts 13: 49).

But opposition continued to grow. People of high standing stirred up persecution against the missionaries until they were eventually forced to leave. We might imagine this to be a devastating blow to them, but instead, Luke, the author of Acts tells us, 'the disciples were filled with joy and with the Holy Spirit' (v 52).

How can this be? Surely, joy is an emotion expressed when things are going well? Yet here Paul and Barnabas are joyous even though things have ended badly. What is this joy that seems to transcend circumstances?

Some people might equate joy with happiness. I read one psychologist's article that suggested happiness can be linked to giving to others, gratitude, being absorbed in something meaningful, even forgiveness. These observations have merit, but we could argue that they only support the notion that the state of being happy depends on external factors, and so it is temporary. When Paul talks about joy in his letters, he seems to be describing something deeper and more permanent.

For example, later in life, Paul recounted some of the challenges he faced over years, throughout his ministry. In the second letter to the Corinthians, he describes hardships, persecutions, stress, calamity, beatings, riots, sleepless nights, hunger and the list goes on.

But even though such times made him, 'sorrowful', he adds that he is, 'yet always rejoicing' (2 Cor 6: 10). Or, as the Passion translation puts it, 'we may suffer, yet in every season we are always found rejoicing'. Throughout his very difficult life, Paul was able to continue rejoicing - he was still able to find and experience joy (see also 2 Cor 7: 4).

There is, of course, an intentionality with Paul. He *chooses* to rejoice, but I don't think this is the same as putting on a brave face. Paul chooses to look upon the one who gives joy. Perhaps at difficult times, he remembered the words of the psalmist in Psalm 16.

In this Psalm, David asks for help, but he also speaks out praise to God (Ps 16: 2). He deliberately sets his attention on the Lord day and night, (v 7 – 8) and he makes a decision to rejoice in verse 9. Then, it seems, he experiences joy, triumphantly ending his psalm with, 'In Your presence is fullness of joy; at Your right hand are pleasures forevermore' (NKJV).

I think this might be part of the secret of experiencing joy: choosing first to rejoice, despite the circumstances, and second, rejoicing over the blessings of heaven that are permanent and unchanging.

Suggested prayer: Take a moment to think about the blessings of Heaven. Reflect on aspects of His creation and start to give thanks for blessings God has given you, past and present. Tell God how you feel about those blessings and express your love to Him. As you do those simple things, you are rejoicing. Try to do this every day.

DAY 78

The Most Creative People on the Planet

I was with a bunch of 11-year-olds recently and we had just read the incredible account of God's Creation in Genesis 1. We stopped at this verse:

'God created mankind in his own image,
in the image of God he created them;
male and female he created them' (Gen 1: 27)

I asked them if they knew what 'image' meant. Most of them didn't seem to. So, I found my phone, took a selfie, and then held it up next to me. I asked them if me and my selfie were the same.

A debate ensued and half of the group said 'yes' while the others said 'no'. The first half were surprised when I agreed with the 'no' verdict that we were not the same. I asked, 'can this picture talk to you like I am talking to you? Can you have a conversation with it?' They got the point and we concluded that me in person is similar to my selfie (my image), but it is not the same.

My next question to the young people was, 'If we are God's image, in what ways are we similar to God?'

We abandoned the idea of us looking the same, but they came out with some great suggestions like - we both have feelings/emotions, and we understand right and wrong. However, I was interested to note that none of them related it back to the passage we had just read and to the one attribute that shouts out the loudest: God is the most amazing creator.

Genesis chapter one is an exuberant celebration of beauty and grandeur, colours and forms; an explosion of invention, soaring from the vast distances of the stars to the fine detail of the tiniest living organism. God's creative ability is mind-boggling to say the least.

And we have been made in His image. So, it is not surprising that the world has been soaked and enriched with art, music, architecture, and language since those first six days at the dawn of time.

Having said that, we know that the story in the third chapter of Genesis reveals a moment when that image was stained with sin. Adam and Eve's intentional disobedience of God had a myriad of consequences, not least their ability to reflect God's holiness. But their creative abilities were deeply affected too. In the generations that followed, people built idols to worship, weapons to kill and palaces and jewelry to enhance their pride.

It wasn't until Jesus walked the earth, that the world again saw, untarnished, the image of God in a human being: 'He is the image of the invisible God', says Paul in Col 1: 15. And we saw it in Jesus' creativity. For example, His parables describing the Kingdom of God are still masterpieces of storytelling today.

Christians have been forgiven for every wrongdoing through Christ's death on the cross, but by the mercy and grace of God, it doesn't end there. The Bible tells us that we are being 'transformed into his (Jesus') likeness' (2 Cor 3: 18). The word, 'likeness' here is often translated as 'image'. As we continue to walk in fellowship with Him, depending on the power of His Spirit and feeding regularly on His Word, we are daily being restored into His image.

So, what does that mean in terms of our creative abilities? Let me suggest this: If we use them for the glory of God and for the benefit of those around us, potentially, I believe that makes us the most creative people on the planet.

Suggested prayer: Have you discovered all the gifts and abilities God has given you? Probably not! Ask Him to keep showing you the new skills and talents that he wants you to find and nurture. Ask the Lord to use every part of you for His glory.

DAY 79

Walking in Reverse

I was talking with a friend the other day.

He had been offered a role in an organisation where his unique abilities and connections would be vital for the next phase of their vision.

He was flattered with the offer but extremely reluctant to accept it. The trouble was, he had worked for the company several years previously and, although under different management back then, he had not found them willing to embrace his ideas. In fact, the feelings of rejection were still quite raw.

The organisation had moved on since that time with the new leadership team taking it in an exciting new direction, but my friend could only see the pain he felt eight years ago.

While we were talking, I found myself thinking of Moses.

Moses had left Egypt out of favour and under a cloud. After a misguided attempt to win justice for a fellow Israelite, he not only felt the rejection of his own people but the sentence of death from his adoptive father – the Pharaoh. Moses had no choice but to close that chapter of his life and move on.

Years later, and now with a wife and family, God called him back, 'I have indeed seen the misery of my people in Egypt… the cry of the Israelites has reached me, and I have seen the way the Egyptians are oppressing them. So now, go. I am sending you to Pharaoh to bring my people the Israelites out of Egypt.' (Ex 3: 7 - 10)

I wonder what went through Moses' mind.

The first question he asks God is, 'Who am I that I should go to Pharaoh and bring the Israelites out of Egypt?' In other words, 'Lord, I burned that bridge decades ago, they didn't want my help then; I'm sure as heck they don't need it now.' But God had to reassure Moses that things were different now: the elders of Israel will listen to him and there's a different Pharaoh on the throne.

A lengthy conversation ensued between the Lord and Moses and the reluctant prophet finally agreed to do the job.

The end of the story is worth noting. Moses led his people out of slavery, away from the threat of the Egyptian army to the mountain of God where the community was effectively reborn as people of the living God.

History as we know it flowed from that moment.

Moses submitted to the pain of revisiting the past and a nation was established amidst miracles and wonders. For God's purposes to move forward, one man had to step back into a place he thought he had walked away from. For Moses, returning to Egypt would have felt like going backwards, opening old wounds, but in God's master plan it was the key to a significant advance of His purposes.

I wonder if God is calling you to return to something or someone. Life may have moved on, but God is a God of history as well as the future and the two are more than linked. In order for God to bear His fruit in and through you in the future, maybe He is calling you to walk through an old familiar door – even if just for a season. God may have unfinished business for you to attend to in order for you to step into the future.

Suggested prayer: Lord, are you calling me to revisit a person, or an unresolved situation? If there are wounds that you want to heal, relationships that you want restored or things that you want me to learn, then please show me how to walk back through that door hand-in-hand with you. Amen.

DAY 80

Eternal Life

What do you imagine Heaven to be like? I remember from my childhood images drawn of angels peacefully strumming harps and sitting on white clouds. Nobody ever explained to me how they stayed up there!

I have sometimes tried to visualize meeting loved ones who have passed away before me, even thinking there may be some sort of small delegation waiting to welcome me to my new home. In my mind's eye, there is a white, warm glow in the undefined environment and happy faces. There is no pain and suffering and everyone gets on.

It's a nice and comforting image, but no-one really knows, of course, what we will see, feel and hear when we arrive in our new bodies. What will define our existence in the days and years to follow? What will life be like in eternity?

John records Jesus' magnificent prayer just before his arrest in John 17 where our Lord says something interesting about eternal life. We might think He would try to describe it, after all, He knows it better than we do. But His focus is not on the structure of Heaven or who we might see. This is how He describes it:

'Now this is eternal life: that they know you, the only true God, and Jesus Christ, whom you have sent' (John 17: 3)

For Jesus, the most important thing about Heaven, about eternal life is that we will know God the Father; and Himself, the second person of the Trinity and our Lord and Saviour.

The thing that strikes me about this is that eternity, therefore, has already started. If we have accepted the free gift of salvation through repentance of sins and faith in the death and resurrection of Christ, then we have started to know God and the best is truly yet to come – knowing Him more and more.

I find it hard to imagine what knowing God more might look like, but if studying His creation is anything to go by, then our God is infinitely complex, beautiful, surprising, and inspiring. So many paintings have been painted, books and songs have been written about Him or stirred by something in His world. Imagine the explosion of fresh music and art, dance, poetry and story as we discover more of the wonder of who He is and what He can do.

Perhaps Heaven (or the new Earth as described in Rev 21: 1) will be like an enormous cultural centre of learning, celebration and creativity, centred around the Source of all Life as we continue to dig into the depths of His heart, what He knows, what He thinks and so much more.

I don't think we are heading toward a boring place. Far from it, and I believe the more we get to know Him here and now, the more we look forward to the life to come.

Suggested prayer: Lord, thank you that because of your Son's sacrificial death on the cross, I have eternal life with you. There will be many new joys, adventures and experiences learning about you and your creation in the life to come, but Lord, I want to start that journey now: growing in my knowledge of you throughout the rest of my time on planet Earth. Amen.

ABOUT KHARIS PUBLISHING

KHARIS PUBLISHING is an independent, traditional publishing house with a core mission to publish impactful books, and channel proceeds into establishing mini-libraries or resource centers for orphanages in developing countries, so these kids will learn to read, dream, and grow. Every time you purchase a book from Kharis Publishing or partner as an author, you are helping give these kids an amazing opportunity to read, dream, and grow. Kharis Publishing is an imprint of Kharis Media LLC. Learn more at https://www.kharispublishing.com.

www.ingramcontent.com/pod-product-compliance
Lightning Source LLC
Chambersburg PA
CBHW070152100426
42743CB00013B/2889